Henry VIII

Very Interesting People

VIP

*Bite-sized biographies of Britain's most
fascinating historical figures*

Henry VIII

Very Interesting People

Eric Ives

OXFORD
UNIVERSITY PRESS

OXFORD
UNIVERSITY PRESS

Great Clarendon Street, Oxford ox2 6DP

Oxford University Press is a department of the University of Oxford.
It furthers the University's objective of excellence in research, scholarship,
and education by publishing worldwide in

Oxford New York

Auckland Cape Town Dar es Salaam Hong Kong Karachi
Kuala Lumpur Madrid Melbourne Mexico City Nairobi
New Delhi Shanghai Taipei Toronto

With offices in

Argentina Austria Brazil Chile Czech Republic France Greece
Guatemala Hungary Italy Japan Poland Portugal Singapore
South Korea Switzerland Thailand Turkey Ukraine Vietnam

Oxford is a registered trade mark of Oxford University Press
in the UK and in certain other countries

Published in the United States
by Oxford University Press Inc., New York

First published in the *Oxford Dictionary of National Biography* 2004
This paperback edition first published 2007

© Oxford University Press 2007

Database right Oxford University Press (maker)

First published 2007

British Library Cataloguing in Publication Data

Data available

Library of Congress Cataloging in Publication Data

Data available

Typeset by SPI Publisher Services, Pondicherry, India
Printed in Great Britain
on acid-free paper by
Clays Ltd, St Ives plc

ISBN 978–0–19–921759–5 (Pbk.)

10 9 8 7 6 5 4 3 2 1

Contents

Preface

Anyone asked to write a biography of Henry VIII knows that he is in for trouble. Grappling with the unique and climactic political, religious, and constitutional events of the reign was difficult enough in 1891 when an article on Henry was written for the first *Dictionary of National Biography*. But since 1945, increased availability of archives and an avalanche of scholarship has transformed our understanding of the period. The invitation I received to write the entry on Henry for the *Oxford Dictionary of National Biography* (2004), and from which this short book derives, was therefore a challenge.

Governing England had always been personal, and hence the monarch should be dominant in the history of every earlier reign—in so far as he can be known. But thanks to the increased range and quality of available documentation, Henry VIII can be known to a depth and his influence determined to an extent impossible with his predecessors. For example, there is no need to guess at motivation with Henry VIII. Under his father, Henry VII, we have to infer the purpose of a statute from its text and even then cannot be sure that it represented the king's will. Under his son we can not only follow the processes of drafting but also much of the politics which lay behind the enactment. An even more striking instance is the religious changes of the reign. Here research has revealed a hitherto unrealized depth of Henry's personal commitment and involvement.

Being made aware of the personal input of a king as never before puts a premium on recovering Henry VIII's character and personality. Psychological profiling is a dangerous business at the best of times, and even more after many hundred of years, but it is unavoidable. So too is consideration of Henry's relations with individuals, and not least his wives and children which, in turn, leads to consideration of his mode of living. Court life has been reclaimed from Hollywood and court culture from connoisseurs. A court was the king and the king was the court.

We have also to recognize that influence was not only one-way—from Henry on policy and government, court and family. The events and the unprecedented changes of his reign meant that Henry's own involvement changed. In particular, the steady expansion of crown activity posed the question: 'how can, or how much longer can, an increasingly complex government continue to depend on the personal input of a single individual?' For good practical reasons, Henry in 1546–7 could not have ruled in the way his father had fifty years earlier. Even more significant, the character of kingship had been revolutionized by Henry's religious changes and in consequence so had his self-image. The distance from 1509 and 'Henry VIII by the grace of God, king', to 1547 and 'Henry VIII by the grace of God, king, defender of the faith and on earth supreme head of the church in England and Ireland' is far more than 38 years.

To write a biography of Henry VIII is, thus, no longer a matter of recounting his life and times. It means calling for the real Henry VIII to stand up.

About the author

Eric Ives is Professor of English History (Emeritus) at the University of Birmingham. He has written on English legal history in the early modern period and more recently on the early Tudor court and politics. In 2001 he was appointed OBE for services to history and Birmingham University. His most recent book is *The Life and Death of Anne Boleyn* (2004).

Abbreviations

CSP Milan	A. B. Hinds, ed., *Calendar of state papers and manuscripts existing in the archives and collections of Milan* (1912)
CSP Spain	G. A. Bergenroth, P. De Gayangos, and others, eds., *Calendar of letters, despatches, and state papers, relating to the negotiations between England and Spain*, 13 vols., The National Archives (1862–1954); M. A. S. Hume, ed., *Calendar of letters and state papers, relating to English affairs, preserved in the archives of Simancas*, 4 vols., The National Archives (1892–9); repr. (1971)
CSP Venice	R. Brown, H. F. Brown, and A. B. Hinds, eds., *Calendar of state papers and manuscripts relating to English affairs, existing in the archives and collections of Venice and in other libraries of northern Italy* (1864–1947)

LP Henry VIII   J. S. Brewer, J. Gairdner, and R. H. Brodie, eds., *Letters and papers, foreign and domestic, of the reign of Henry VIII*, 23 vols. in 38 (1862–1932); repr. (1965)

Rymer, *Foedera*   T. Rymer and R. Sanderson, eds., *Foedera, conventiones, literae et cuiuscunque generis acta publica inter reges Angliae et alios quosvis imperatores, reges, pontifices, principes, vel communitates*, 20 vols. (1704–35); 2nd edn, 20 vols. (1726–35); 3rd edn, 10 vols. (1739–45); new edn, ed. A. Clarke, J. Caley, and F. Holbrooke, 4 vols., Record Commissions, 50 (1816–69); facs. of 3rd edn (1967)

Upbringing and inheritance, 1491–1514

Henry VIII (1491–1547),

king of England and Ireland, was the second surviving son of Henry VII (1457–1509) and his wife, Elizabeth (1466–1503), eldest child of Edward IV. He was born at Greenwich on 28 June 1491 and baptized in the church of the Observant friars there, by Richard Fox, then bishop of Exeter.

Childhood and education

Although created duke of York on 31 October 1494, Henry's childhood was overshadowed by his brother Arthur (1486–1502), prince of Wales and five years his senior. Indeed, Henry's first known public appearance was at the marriage of Arthur and his Spanish bride, Katherine (1485–1536), daughter of Ferdinand of Aragon and Isabella of Castile, on 14 November 1501, when the ten-year-old led their wedding procession through London. Twenty weeks later Henry's status and expectations were transformed by the death of Arthur on 2 April 1502. In October he was created duke of Cornwall and in February 1503 prince of Wales and earl of Chester.

Details of Henry's education are sparse, but it probably resembled that of his brother, Prince Arthur. This was based on the classics and covered grammar, poetry, rhetoric and ethics, and a good deal of history. Henry's first tutor was the poet John Skelton. Lord Herbert of Cherbury claimed that Henry was initially destined for the see of Canterbury but cited no evidence, and since he became heir to the throne at the age he did, any such intention would have had little effect on his training. That a career in the church was ever thought of seems unlikely, given the lands and offices granted to Henry at the age of three to support the dukedom of York. Herbert's suggestion was probably an attempt to account for the very considerable interest in and knowledge of theology which the adult Henry showed, before as well as after his dispute with Rome.

A remark of Thomas More that Henry was nourished on philosophy and the Nine Muses suggests that his education had a humanist cast, and comments by Erasmus (who met the boy and corresponded with him) confirm this. Henry spoke French and Latin well, understood Italian and learned some Spanish. He was very well read and had real, if not profound, intellectual interests. Genuine curiosity made him fascinated with scientific instruments, maps, and astronomy. The adult Henry resembled his grandfather Edward IV, reaching a height of 6 feet 2 inches; at twenty-one his waist was 32 inches. He had a fair complexion and his hair inclined to ginger. He could dominate any gathering and was extrovert, affable, and charming. Full of energy and proud of his athleticism, Henry cast himself above all in a military role and had a passion for weapons and fortifications. A fine horseman and an excellent archer, he was an enthusiast for those two substitutes for war: hunting and the tournament. In 1511 he took the first steps which led in 1515 to the organization of the royal armouries at Greenwich to equip himself and his courtiers to fight at the barriers and to joust.

This was Henry as his subjects saw him, but the years would reveal that behind this apparent extroversion and good humour was a highly complex individual. How much of the royal psychology was the product of upbringing it is possible only to speculate. Erasmus was much taken with the eight-year-old Henry and a portrait bust attributed to Guido Mazzoni which probably represents him at the same age shows a happy child, engaged and responsive. Arthur's death possibly affected Henry's status more than his emotions, but his mother's death early the next year left a wound which he recalled years later, though it is impossible to tell whether that was a genuine memory from the age of eleven, or merely a Renaissance trope. There have been suggestions that Henry's grandmother Lady Margaret Beaufort had some influence on his upbringing, but precisely how is unclear and she was to die only two months after his accession.

Information on Henry's relations with his somewhat withdrawn and controlled father is mixed. His cousin Reginald Pole claimed that Henry VII showed no affection to his heir and it is true that all hopes had been focused on Prince Arthur. In contrast to his elder brother, Henry was given no public authority and the Spanish diplomat Fuensalida wrote of a boy kept under a minute supervision more suited to a girl, and 'so subjected that he does not speak a word except in response to what the King asks him' (*Correspondencia de … Fuensalida*, 449). Yet with only one of Henry VII's sons left alive, this might well be simple protectiveness (which could explain other reports of teenage rebellion). That it was less than excessive is clear from reports in these same diplomatic sources of the prince spending much of his last summer of freedom in the tilt-yard at Richmond, on at least one occasion performing for his father.

The demands of kingship

Henry VIII succeeded to a monarchy in which the ruler was directly responsible for policy and directly involved in the business of government. An agenda for his attention might include fifty items and his signature would be needed several times a day. Monarchy was personal. Everything, therefore, depended on the king's willingness to devote himself to business. Henry VII had been a model in this respect, but not his son. Henry VIII frequently behaved as though he wanted government to take care of itself. His favourite hours for business were during morning mass and before bed. Most state papers were read to or summarized for him and he did almost all his work by word of mouth. Only on issues which engaged him personally was he willing to become fully committed.

On the other hand, Henry was not willing to delegate consistently. He always reserved to himself the freedom to intervene as and when he wanted. The consequence was not only that decisions might have to wait for the king to return from hunting or to be in the mood for work, but that Henry might decide to initiate action independently and even contradict steps already put in hand. These habits of work also exacerbated a problem inherent in personal monarchy: that the physical locus of policy and government was necessarily the royal household, but that this household was peripatetic. Henry's court moved (as did other great households in the days of poor sanitation), from palace to palace, or, in somewhat reduced numbers, accompanied him in summer and autumn on a progress through southern England which could last as much as five months. The result was a separation between the king and the royal administrative institutions which depended on his decisions and were effectively static in Westminster and London. For example, how during the law terms could counsellors be present to advise the ruler when they were required to sit in star chamber, or again, what were counsellors at Westminster to do when instructed to spend money they knew they did not have?

The need to accommodate Henry VIII's particular version of personal monarchy explains much in the story of his reign. In essence there were two options. The first was that the royal council should attempt to provide some regularity and the second that a minister should take over as chief executive, leaving the king as overall director. Neither met the difficulties fully and the story of the reign is of oscillation as the options were tried in turn and successively broke down.

At the start of the reign the conciliar option was in place, effectively inherited from Henry's father. The grey heads in royal service were happy to see their inexperienced new master busy with first his marriage on 11 June to his brother's widow, Katherine of Aragon, and then a magnificent joint coronation on 24 June. Behind the scenes, however, there had been a coup. Henry VII's death had been kept a close secret for forty-eight hours to allow aristocratic counsellors to put a stop to the old king's mechanism of financial terror, arrest his principal agents, Richard Empson and Edmund Dudley, and secure a general pardon to wipe out past vulnerabilities. It was the first of the factional confrontations which would become so characteristic of the reign.

Henry's priority in these early years was to establish his European status and reputation by war against the traditional enemy, France. However, a majority of the council adhered to his father's preference for peace and there was also a need to find allies, so that it was not until 1512 that war was declared. A year of failed expeditions followed (not least because of treachery by his father-in-law and supposed ally, Ferdinand), but in 1513 Henry himself led an army into the Low Countries. There, with minimum support from another ally, Maximilian I, the holy Roman emperor, the English won the scrambling cavalry action known as the battle of the Spurs and captured Thérouanne and Tournai from the French. Henry lived on the fame of this success for the rest of his life but in his absence a far more significant victory was won by the earl of Surrey over the Scots at Flodden which left their king dead in the field. Further campaigning in 1514 was, however, brought to a halt following the desertion of his allies, and under pressure from the pope Henry himself made peace with France and sealed it by marrying his sister Mary (1496–1533) to the decrepit French king, Louis XII.

After five years on the throne, conciliar administration was beginning to wear thin. Henry felt more able to decide for himself and round him was growing up a circle of courtiers and advisers who were his own. Several of the men whom, as a young king, he had looked up to had been casualties during the war, and Henry now began to prefer the company of younger men who looked up to him. And the change was in more than personnel. In each royal residence Henry, like his father, occupied a private suite insulated from the ceremonial side of the court. However, while Henry VII had been perfectly prepared to be attended in this 'privy chamber' by servants, his son wanted the company of these new companions, and by the time the first decade of his reign was over, a new staffing pattern had emerged which surrounded him with 'gentlemen' and 'grooms of the privy chamber' who, as well as attending to his needs, provided him with a social life. They were headed by 'the groom of the close stool', his most intimate attendant, who doubled in the post of chief gentleman of the privy chamber. This availability of a private staff of gentlemen directly dependent on him allowed a king who wished to do so to bypass the usual channels and take direct action, as, for example, when arresting both the duke of Buckingham and Cardinal Wolsey. The reverse, however, was that closeness to the king gave the privy chamber the potential for real political importance, with the staff able to meddle in the exercise of patronage and to attempt to sway royal thinking. The groom of the stool, in particular, could be influential in assisting or discouraging access to the king.

Wolsey as royal minister, 1514–1530

2

The king's minister

The French war of 1512–14 saw Thomas Wolsey emerge from the pack of royal counsellors as someone who could offer Henry the option of ruling through a principal minister rather than at first hand through a council. It was not only because of his boundless energy and undoubted ability, but because Wolsey saw it as his function (and guarantee of his continued enjoyment of success and power) to give the king what he wanted, or could be persuaded that he did want. Collectively the other royal counsellors were reduced to giving advice only when Henry and Wolsey wished and to discharging the council's judicial work, although individually they continued to manage particular activities as they had under Henry VII. Wolsey reported to Henry in person, usually at least once a week, and also by letter. A small group of counsellors Wolsey could trust was also always in attendance at court.

For a decade and more, working through Wolsey allowed Henry to rule in the way he wanted. It led some contemporaries (and later historians) to the illusion that the minister was in charge—hence talk of him as 'the person who rules both the king and the kingdom' (*CSP Venice*, 1509–19, 569). In reality, however, the collaboration ensured that Henry was consulted on everything important and, should he wish, could initiate, but was left free of detail and day-to-day routine. George Cavendish, Wolsey's gentleman usher, described the system from firsthand observation. The minister:

> wold first make the king privye of all suche matters (as shold passe throughe [the council's] handes) byfore he wold procede to the fynyssheng or determynyng of the same, whos mynd and pleasure he wold fullfyll and followe to the uttermost wherewith the king was wonderly pleased. (Cavendish, 12)

Judging from the state papers which have survived from Wolsey's ministry, Henry's principal interest in these years was diplomacy—how to place England in relation to the shifting context of the Italian wars. The policy pursued by the minister (at Henry's instigation Wolsey was elected archbishop of York in 1514, then appointed cardinal in 1515, and in 1518 papal legate a latere) has been interpreted variously as support for the Holy See in the hope of himself becoming pope, pursuit of a balance of power, searching for peace (in part for reasons of principle), and personal self-advancement. A simpler explanation is suggested by the situation in Europe. There Charles V, Katherine's nephew, had united the Habsburg lands and the holy Roman empire with the kingdoms of Spain and its American empire, and he was engaged in great-power rivalry with François I of France. In comparison England was significantly inferior—the population of France was six times greater and Charles V's income was seven times larger than Henry's. Wolsey's object, therefore, was to manoeuvre in such a way as to achieve equivalent status for Henry, in effect to enable England to punch far above its weight. The cardinal's greatest triumph was the treaty signed in London in 1518 which brought together the major European powers and twenty smaller ones in an alliance for 'universal peace'. Subsequently Charles V accepted an invitation to discussions in London in May 1520, and the next month Henry met François I at Ardres, on the border between France and English-occupied Calais. Both summits were made occasions for magnificence and especially the latter, known thereafter, because of the finery worn for the occasion, as the Field of Cloth of Gold.

Underneath the ostensible harmony 'concluded in England' (*CSP Venice*, 1509–19, 458) there were, however, increasing signs of the return of Franco-imperial rivalry over Italy, a development which left Henry, 'the arbiter of Europe', on the sidelines. He therefore followed the 1520 meeting with François I with a second and more businesslike meeting with Charles which eventually led to England going to war with France in 1522 as an ally of the emperor. What followed exposed the hollowness of Henry's pretensions to big-power status. Raids into northern France in 1522 and 1523 achieved nothing, money ran out, and when Charles captured François on 23 February 1525 at the battle of Pavia, the emperor refused to countenance a wild proposal by Henry to divide France between them. Unable to gain any kudos as Charles's ally, England thereupon made peace with France and when the pope put together the Holy League of Cognac to try to contain imperial power, Henry became its 'protector'. Shortage of funds ruled out any more positive involvement.

In contrast to what may to later minds appear the charade of this foreign posturing, the collaboration of Henry and Wolsey in domestic affairs did have long-term significance. The coup against Henry VII's methods which had opened the reign had significantly weakened royal finances, notably by reducing the income of the crown estates. This was made worse by the expense of foreign war—the war with France in 1512–14 cost about £1,000,000, perhaps ten times Henry's normal revenue. The sequel was a determined and partially successful campaign to increase royal revenues from taxation. In 1515 progress was made on developing the parliamentary subsidy, a tax assessed on real wealth in place of the older system of fixed levies. In 1522 a 'general proscription' or survey was carried out, allegedly to measure military preparedness, and the data collected was used to assess and levy a non-parliamentary forced loan. The survey was also used to assess the subsidy of 1523–5 and succeeded in taxing perhaps 90 per cent of rural households and up to two-thirds of townsmen. It became the model for future years. The country grumbled, but it was only when the crown added a call for a 'benevolence' in 1525, the so-called 'amicable grant', that it encountered serious resistance where it mattered, in London, the home counties, and East Anglia. Thanks to his system of ruling at one remove, Henry was able to claim ignorance of the demand, make tactful concessions, and leave Wolsey to take the blame publicly.

Another consequence of the palace coup on Henry VII's death had been the partial relaxation of his stern disciplining of élite misconduct. In 1516, therefore, his son presided at a special council meeting where Wolsey announced a return to the policy of 'indifferent justice' and the king himself provided an object lesson by sending the fifth earl of Northumberland to the Fleet prison. The following year saw riots in London against immigrant Flemish workers, the 'Evil May Day', with some fourteen or so offenders being hanged and the remainder paraded in Westminster Hall before the king and queen, the lords, and the council. Wolsey berated both the city government and the rioters and called for more executions but on Queen Katherine's petition (clearly arranged in advance) Henry exercised the prerogative of mercy. Two years later the king appeared in council to deal with Sir William Bulmer who despite being a royal officer had nevertheless accepted a retainer from the third duke of Buckingham.

The royal endorsement of the 'law and order' policy given by Henry's appearance at these set pieces was followed up by Wolsey in a large number of less high-profile cases pursued through the routine legal machinery. Landowners fell foul of him particularly over breaches of the statutes prohibiting the enclosure and conversion of arable land for pasture. It would, however, be wrong to suggest that Henry had sanctioned an assault on the country's élite, a supposition frequently labelled as 'the attack on over-mighty subjects'. Royal power depended on the men of power using their social authority to serve the state, most especially the military potential of their tenants and 'well-wishers'—their *manred*. In particular a peerage was essential to monarchy. It provided a majority of counsellors, was the bedrock of royal influence in parliament and created the setting for royal magnificence, and was a reservoir of higher commanders in war. Henry 'inherited' forty-two peers and in his first twenty years created a further thirteen and promoted six more. This was followed in 1529 by seven more creations and three promotions. Thereafter creations and/or promotions took place almost every year. Certainly individuals were prosecuted, liberties and rights questioned, but always in relation to personal conduct or perceived unreliability. The most famous example of this was the duke of Buckingham, whose unwise behaviour suggested disaffection and led to his execution in 1521.

The danger which Buckingham represented was undoubtedly exaggerated in Henry's mind by a concern which was beginning to worry him more and more—the lack of a son to succeed him. Katherine's first child miscarried and the second, Prince Henry (born on new year's day 1511) survived only a matter of days. Only one of four further conceptions was successful—the birth of Princess Mary (later Mary I) in 1516—and in 1519 (the year of Katherine's last pregnancy) the king was anxious enough to bring physicians over from Spain to examine his wife, who at thirty-four was approaching her last years of fertility.

Katherine clearly had problems in bringing pregnancies to full term but six pregnancies in ten years of marriage show that the couple also had difficulty in achieving conception. Henry must then have taken comfort from the birth to Elizabeth Blount, also in 1519, of an illegitimate son, Henry Fitzroy. The king had no qualms in acknowledging the boy and in 1525 he was created duke of Richmond and Somerset. These peerages were closely associated with the Tudor family and some at the time (and since) have believed that Henry was toying with the idea of legitimating Richmond as heir apparent; Katherine allegedly took the news very badly. Henry's more immediate motive was probably the desire to make use of his son as a surrogate— a month after the investiture Richmond was made warden-general of the Scottish marches—but if the possibility of the boy succeeding him was in the king's mind at all, the risk that would involve is only further evidence of anxiety about the future. Time was now not on Henry's side. He was thirty-four. His grandfathers had died aged twenty-six and forty-one. His father had died aged fifty-two. In 1524 the king had abandoned intercourse with Katherine, and England, for the first time since the early twelfth century, was heading for a female on the throne. As the daughter of Isabella of Castile, Katherine saw no problem, but to Henry and his subjects it was a frightening prospect. The only escape would be by a son of a second marriage—and this required either the death of Katherine or the ending of her marriage to Henry. Moreover, unless that son was born in the near future he would succeed as a minor, and the success record of royal minors was bleak.

Katherine, though childless, was in good health, but breaking a marriage for dynastic reasons was by no means an impossibility. 'Divorce' in its modern meaning was not allowed under canon law, but 'annulment'—a declaration that no valid marriage had been contracted—was a real option, generally on the ground of consanguinity which was construed much more strictly than today. Katherine's marriage to Henry had certainly fallen into the prohibited category, since by her union with his brother Arthur she was held to have become Henry's sister and so quite out of the question as a wife. However, the church also claimed the power to condone potential defects revealed in advance, and Pope Julius II had issued a papal bull allowing Katherine and Henry to marry despite their relationship. For his marriage to Katherine to be annulled, that dispensation had to be impugned.

There is evidence that Henry had long had niggling doubts about the lawfulness of his marriage but, with Wolsey's connivance, the first secret steps towards an annulment were not taken until May 1527. It was later claimed that the king's doubts had been aroused by questions asked during the previous winter in the negotiations for a marriage between Princess Mary and François I's second son, but though that may have been so, it was just what was needed to crystallize Henry's innermost

anxieties. He was meticulous in his religious duties—God must
be on his side—yet his children continued to die in the womb
or in infancy. And did not Leviticus 20: 21 say that if a man had
sexual relations with his brother's wife, they would be childless?

What part did Anne Boleyn (c.1500–1536) play in Henry's decision? He seems to have been pursuing her from the early part
of 1526, but the first sign that she had agreed to marry him was
an application to Pope Clement VII for the two of them to be
dispensed which was sent off in August 1527. The letters the
king wrote to Anne in 1527 and 1528 can be variously interpreted, but the probable resolution is that his original object
had been to secure her as his mistress in succession to her sister
Mary, with whom he had enjoyed a childless relationship in the
early 1520s. Only after he had decided to seek an annulment
did Anne's refusal of what seems to have been his invitation
to become *maîtresse en titre* suggest that she would be the
ideal second wife instead of a French princess as Wolsey had
assumed.

Henry and Anne clearly expected to wed within months, but
five and a half years' frustration lay ahead. The delay was
in part caused by the international situation. The victory of
Charles V at Pavia in 1525 and the sack of Rome two years
later had put Katherine of Aragon's nephew on the way to a
mastery of Italy. The pope still had hopes of the League of
Cognac but caution removed all incentive to burn his boats by
accommodating Henry. He therefore deliberately deceived the
king, making a series of apparent concessions while secretly
doing everything possible to hold matters up. In all fairness
to Clement it must also be said that he was ill-informed.
The opinion in Europe was that all Henry wanted was a
new bedmate in place of his ageing, barren, and increasingly

lachrymose wife. Time, therefore, would solve the problem: Anne would pass into the royal bed and later out of it to a suitably discreet marriage, or Katherine would solve the problem by dying. Henry's obstinate morality was something which a pope in Renaissance Rome found hard to understand.

The pope's reluctance was, moreover, also prompted by the real legal difficulties which annulment presented. To Henry, God's commands might be blindingly obvious. His marriage to Katherine was contrary to divine law as stated in the Bible and therefore could not be set aside. It was said that 'an angel descending from Heaven would be unable to persuade him otherwise' (*LP Henry VIII*, 4/2, no. 4858). But not only did Henry's conviction require the pope to accept that Julius II had exceeded his authority in issuing the original dispensation, Clement had good reason to believe that the king had got hold of the wrong biblical text. The passage Henry relied on appeared to refer not to a brother's widow but to a brother's wife and so be a prohibition on adultery. Moreover, verse 5 of Deuteronomy 25 specifically instructed a brother to marry his widowed sister-in-law if she had had no sons in order to provide a surrogate heir for his dead sibling. Henry's obstinate fixation on Leviticus and the explanation it provided for his childlessness drove him deeper and deeper into a legal and exegetical cul-de-sac from which the only escape would be to break down the barrier of papal authority.

Stalemate and the death of Wolsey, 1527–1530

The struggle for the annulment falls into three phases, 1527 to 1529, 1529 to 1530, and 1530 to 1533. In the first, royal policy was directed by Wolsey and ended with the minister becoming the first casualty of the king's Great Matter. The cardinal had to fight on three fronts. In international affairs he strove to free the pope from the emperor's domination by reducing the imperial position in Italy. At Rome he negotiated tirelessly for the decision Henry wanted. At home he struggled to retain royal favour and the control of policy despite continuing setbacks which gave opportunity to his enemies at court.

Wolsey's diplomatic options were restricted by royal financial weakness and the fact that England's economic ties with the Low Countries made significant direct action against Charles impracticable—the war declared early in 1528 had to be abandoned within weeks. Initial French moves did raise some hope that the pope would evade dependence on Charles but these were followed in 1528 by reverses in the south of Italy, and in June 1529 by defeat at the battle of Landriano and expulsion from the north. On 29 June Clement VII signed the treaty of Barcelona with Charles which recognized the emperor's position in Italy and, by implication, his own future as an imperial satellite. Five days afterwards the efforts of François I's mother, Louise of Savoy, and Charles's aunt, Margaret of Austria, brought about the 'Ladies Peace' (treaty of Cambrai) by which France agreed to abandon its claims to Italy. England was effectively ignored and Wolsey was left without diplomatic leverage.

In the meantime, at Rome Henry's agents had been pursuing his suit. Initial attempts to keep Katherine in ignorance failed, and in July 1527 the queen alerted both emperor and pope to her side of the story which was that her marriage with Arthur was void because never consummated. Everything thereafter would depend on where the case would be decided and in December 1527 Henry sent a mission to Rome requesting a legatine commission empowering Wolsey and

Lorenzo Campeggi or Campeggio, cardinal protector of England and bishop of Salisbury *in commendam*, to hear and settle the case in England. Successive papal commissions were issued throughout 1528, but none with power to make the final binding decision which Henry had to have to be secure. In October 1528 Campeggi eventually arrived in England and with a convincing commission, but also with orders that it should not be used (he later destroyed it) and a secret mandate to procrastinate. Eventually a legatine court did open at Blackfriars in June 1529. Katherine formally appealed to Rome and on 21 June the confrontation took place between king and queen later made famous by Shakespeare. Katherine appealed to Henry to admit that she was a virgin when she married him, and torn between a public confrontation and remaining silent, or perhaps between a fatal truth and a lie no one would believe, Henry said nothing and the queen walked out. The one-sided hearing dragged on until Campeggi announced that the court must keep Roman law terms and on 31 July adjourned business until October.

Through all these delays, and especially during 1529, Wolsey had also been fighting to maintain his position. The personal nature of the annulment suit encouraged Henry into one of his periodic bouts of activity and he also began to listen to other advisers as well. When, in January 1529, there was still no progress despite Campeggi's arriving three months before, Anne Boleyn decided that Wolsey was complicit and she abandoned her previous reliance on him. Her new hostility put Henry's continuing confidence in the cardinal under question and a mixed bag of public figures began to come together united by dislike of the minister, but only a few of them positive Boleyn supporters. A dossier of complaints against Wolsey was prepared, and on the collapse of the Blackfriars court this was submitted to the king. Henry, however, was unable to break free of fifteen years of dependence on the cardinal and took no action. It was only at the end of August when Wolsey began to advise against the alliance with France which Henry saw as crucial to breaking the impasse over the marriage that the cardinal really lost favour. He recovered somewhat after a positive meeting with Henry at Grafton on 19 September, but three weeks later the king yielded to the cardinal's critics and allowed him to be charged in the court of king's bench with the offence of *praemunire*—that is, breaching the fourteenth-century statutes restricting papal authority in England. Even that decision may, paradoxically, have been motivated by Henry's desire to protect Wolsey; parliament had been summoned for November and this threatened an alternative and far worse danger—an act of attainder. Wolsey pleaded guilty, was dismissed as chancellor, and sent into comfortable house arrest.

With the fall of Wolsey the problem of the annulment passed to Henry and to the cardinal's replacements headed by Anne Boleyn's uncle, Thomas Howard, third duke of Norfolk. No one had much idea what to do, and the real concern of the new advisers was to prevent Wolsey returning to the side of a king who had already been heard to mutter 'every day I miss the cardinal of York more and more' (*CSP Milan*, 530). Fortunately for them, death removed that danger on 29 November 1530. The king's own reaction to Blackfriars had been to bluster. According to the imperial ambassador, Henry threatened that if Clement VII did not accommodate him, he 'would denounce the pope as a heretic and marry whom he pleased' (*CSP Spain*, 1529–30, 224). Although parliament, the accepted forum for national consensus, had been called, nothing relevant to the annulment suit could be found for it to do. As for the Roman curia, the royal cause dragged on there with minimal progress; indeed, since Henry could count no trial outside England a certainty, his agents actively encouraged delay. The only positive step was implementing a casual suggestion by a Cambridge academic named Thomas Cranmer that the universities of Europe should be consulted, a venture which cost Henry a good deal in bribes but produced eight favourable opinions and a mass of potentially relevant documents. Very clearly neither the king nor his post-Wolsey counsellors had a coherent strategy, still less had decided to 'go it alone'. Henry's only notion was to turn his threats into action; bullying the English church would make the pope realize that Henry was serious! In June 1530 a meeting of English notables, clerical and lay, was called to support a national petition to Rome pleading for an immediate verdict in the king's favour and uttering further dire but vague menaces. In the autumn fifteen leading members of the church hierarchy were charged with complicity in Wolsey's offences.

New ideas and a new minister, 1530–1532

The headship of the church

In the latter part of 1530 a dramatic change comes over the king's Great Matter. For example, in October Henry instructed his agents at Rome to deny the right of the pope to consider Katherine's appeal because 'in [our kingdom] we are supreme and so rule that we recognise no superior...and he who acknowledges no superior has the power to prohibit all appeals by his subjects' (*State Papers, Henry VIII*, 7.262). In January 1531 words became action. Henry declared that in exercising the jurisdiction of the church courts the English clergy had fallen 'into divers dangers of his laws' and demanded that convocation should raise £100,000 to purchase a pardon. The church agreed to pay, but the king then made further demands, insisting that the church should admit three principles: that he was 'the only protector and supreme head of the English church and clergy', that God had committed to him a 'cure' ('care') of souls (in other words that he possessed a spiritual character and function), and that the church could only enjoy powers 'which do not disparage the regal authority and laws' (Wilkins, 3.257). This time convocation did not give way and the king had to compromise. On the first point the crown offered the ambiguous qualification 'as far as the law of Christ allows' and the king's claim to a quasi-spiritual 'cure of souls' was watered down (Scarisbrick, 'The pardon of the clergy', 34). The issue of church authority was fudged. Even so there was considerable local opposition in the dioceses, with protests of loyalty to Rome, which the crown met with further *praemunire* charges.

Where had the king's new assertiveness come from? Not from his own thinking. When his interest was engaged, Henry was capable of intellectual effort. In 1521 he had published the *Assertio septem sacramentorum*, a rebuttal of Martin Luther's anti-papal diatribe *De captivitate Babylonica*, which earned him the title 'Defender of the Faith'. Yet although effective at one level, the book does not suggest that the king had an original mind. Its affirmation of papal supremacy and condemnation of schism is quite conventional. It is also clear that the king had relied on help. Very probably a team did the preliminary work, leaving Henry to give the final touches to a book made unusual only by reason of the identity of the author. It was the same subsequently, when he was wrestling with his matrimonial dilemma. He told Anne Boleyn in 1528 how four hours work on 'his book' had given him a headache (Stemmler, xiv).

What had given Henry this new confidence was again the work of other men. The study of canon law, theology, and the opinions of the European universities had not stopped with the collapse of the Blackfriars trial. In November 1531 Thomas Cranmer was able to publish *The Determinations of the Most Famous and Excellent Universities*, an elaboration of the case put to the legatine court which achieved a new stage in menace by asserting that 'the duty of a loving and a devout bishop [was] to withstand the Pope openly to his face' for failing to enforce obedience to God in matrimonial cases such as Henry's (Sturtz and Murphy, 265). At the same time researchers had been ransacking biblical, patristic, and later evidence on the issue of papal jurisdiction. The scholars involved here were led by the king's future almoner, Edward Fox, and probably again included Cranmer. By August 1530 their report was in Henry's hands, under the inconvenient label, *Collectanea satis copiosa*. This demonstrated—or claimed to demonstrate—that there was simply no warrant for the centuries-old assumption that the pope was supreme in spiritual matters. The king possessed by divine gift, imperial authority (*imperium*), so that instead of the old theory of 'two swords'—temporal and spiritual authority in the hands of king and pope respectively—both swords belonged to the king. He was the true 'Vicar of God'.

Fox and Cranmer were very much under Boleyn patronage, but Anne herself introduced Henry to further revolutionary ideas which were circulating in Germany about the true place and role of the ruler in God's scheme of things. These had been given currency in England in *The Obedience of the Christian Man*, published in October 1528 by the reformist exile and Bible translator, William Tyndale. Anne had obtained a copy soon after publication and she lent it to Henry with the relevant passages already marked. Tyndale asserted that for princes to submit to the power of the church was not only 'a shame above all shames and a notorious thing' but an inversion of the divine order. 'One king, one law is God's ordinance in every realm' (*Tyndale's Works*, 1.206–7, 240). Henry's response was, 'This is a book for me, and all kings to read' (Nichols, 57).

That such radical ideas rang a bell with the author of something as orthodox as *Assertio septem sacramentorum* was not merely because they suggested a novel way to get what he wanted. In 1515, as his response shows in the affair of Richard Hunne—a dispute over church rights in London—Henry was already highly sensitized on the matter of his God-given authority, particularly encroachments by the church. In 1519 he declared ecclesiastical rights of sanctuary to be an encroachment on royal authority which he would reform unilaterally. Thus far he may merely have been asserting the traditional right of the temporal to delimit the spiritual, but the difficulties of the king's Great Matter inevitably forced Henry to ask, 'what does it mean to be a king under God?' If he was, as he described himself in a letter of 1520 'Soveraigne Lorde and Prince' and 'of our absolute power . . . above the lawes', and if it

> so moche toucheth our honour to conserve our rightfull inheritaunce that We neither may ne woll suffre any Prince, of what soever preheminence he bee, to usurpe or detaigne any parte therof, but, by our puysaunce, to represse suche usurpacion and detencion (*State Papers, Henry VIII*, 3.53)

it was incongruous in the extreme to find himself a rejected suppliant at Rome.

The headship of the church, and the rise of Thomas Cromwell

Despite the attractiveness of the radical option and his willingness to use it as a threat, Henry was reluctant to go all the way with the programme of Anne and her supporters— hence his failure to press home the attack in the pardon of the clergy. Behind him was a lifetime of posing as a loyal son of the church. His comments on the margins of the *Collectanea* show that its thesis seemed too good to be true, and he immediately sent agents abroad to ransack foreign libraries for further evidence to establish that this imperial authority was a reality and was truly independent of the pope. There was also the question of what procedure would legitimate a resumption of such authority. Christopher St German of the Middle Temple was advising Henry that statute did provide a valid basis for legislating on ecclesiastical matters because 'the king in parliament [is] the high sovereign over the people which hath not only charge on the bodies but also on the souls of his subjects' (*St German's Doctor and Student*, 327). Yet was parliament really competent to overturn the objection that, in the words of Thomas More, the supreme government of the church 'may no temporal prince presume by any law to take upon him, as rightfully belonging to the See of Rome, a spiritual pre-eminence [granted] by the mouth of our Saviour himself personally present upon earth?' (Roper, ed. Sylvester and Harding, 248).

The international situation also suggested caution. Charles V, for once at peace with France, was a potential threat. François I promised support, but since he was bidding for papal favour on his own account, that help might not extend to an open breach with Clement. François, indeed, might be in a position to achieve an alternative solution by persuading the pope to compromise, and a papally endorsed annulment would give Anne and her expected offspring the great advantage of being accepted Europe-wide. English opposition was also becoming more vocal. At first this came from the clergy, particularly Katherine's champions, but more and more there were signs of unease in the country at large. Hostile placards appeared in London and the king's problems became a matter of popular debate. Earlier soundings had made clear that a unilateral English solution to the impasse was unacceptable to the nobility. The court became polarized and before the year was out, so too the royal council, with Sir Thomas More (Wolsey's successor as lord chancellor) doing all he could to frustrate the radicals.

The growing confidence of the conservatives was evident in the third session of parliament which assembled in January 1532. The second session, which had met in January 1531, had done nothing for the king's problem except to enact the pardon of the clergy. The duke of Norfolk and the other counsellors now realized matters could wait no longer. Might financial pressure on the pope do the trick? A bill was drafted to put an end to the pope's principal source of revenue from England, the payment of annates, in theory the first year's income of newly appointed members of the hierarchy. The House of Lords refused to entertain the idea and the crown offered to compromise by suspending operation of the bill for an unstated period. Even so, to get that emasculated version through the house, Henry had to appear in person on three occasions. The Commons was equally difficult, forcing the crown to specify that the period of suspension would be a full year and to sanction the continued payment to Rome of five shillings in the pound 'for the pains and labours taken' there. Moreover, the bill was approved only after the king had again arrived in person—he engineered a division, the earliest example of the procedure. Conservatives also blocked other moves by Norfolk. Archbishop William Warham refused to defy the pope, and when the duke tried out the arguments of the *Collectanea* on a group of his supporters he was turned down flat.

If the king and his counsellors were frustrated, so too was Anne Boleyn. Only the radical solution would save the day, but how could royal doubts and conservative resistance be overcome? It is here that another key player entered the scene, Thomas Cromwell. A protégé of Wolsey, Cromwell had been in touch with Anne since 1529 and had quickly absorbed radical ideas. By the opening of 1531 he had been sworn a member of the royal council—indeed, the Trojan Horse formula 'as far as the law of Christ allows' may have been his. He was not yet the supreme policy maker he was to become, but he was a parliamentary expert and a first rate political tactician.

The issue which Cromwell saw he could exploit was agitation in the Commons about church officers abusing their authority over lay people. This had been an issue in the first session, and since then a campaign waged by Thomas More against so-called 'heretics' had raised the temperature. Cromwell responded to this concern by drafting for the Commons a petition cataloguing the faults of the ecclesiastical judges, the so-called 'supplication against the ordinaries'. The opening complaint was a direct challenge to the independent legal status of the church and the supplication ended with an appeal to the king as 'the only head, sovereign lord, protector and defender of both the said parties, in whom and by whom the only sole redress, reformation and remedy herein absolutely rests and remains', in other words a thinly veiled reference to his supreme headship (Bray, 56).

It is unlikely that Henry recognized the supplication as a subtle way to test the meaning of a supreme headship 'as far as the law of Christ allowed'. To Henry the matter was plain; after all, as he told Bishop Tunstal, 'words were ordained to signify things, and cannot therefore by sinister interpretation alter the truth of them' (Wilkins, 3.762). He therefore simply informed the delegation of the Commons which presented the supplication that he would send it to convocation for comment. Instead, the MPs discovered that what was then uppermost in the king's mind was another issue, the loss which his feudal rights of wardship and livery were sustaining from the popularity of 'the use', a legal device which enabled tenants-in-chief to evade payment by effectively putting land in trust. The Lords had accepted a compromise Henry had offered in 1529 but when a bill was put to the Commons in 1532, the king suffered a blank refusal. The warning the members were given was entirely in character: 'I assure you, if you wyll not take some reasonable ende now when it is offered, I wyll serche out the extremitie of the lawe, and then wyll I not offre you so moche agayne' (Hall, 785).

If Henry did not recognize the time bomb in the supplication, neither did convocation. It called on Henry's favourite bishop, Stephen Gardiner, to reply and he walked straight into the trap. He wrote:

> We take our authority of making of laws to be grounded upon the Scripture of God and the determination of Holy Church, which must also be a rule and square to try the justice and righteousness of all laws, as well spiritual as temporal.

If friction occurred, the church would conform its law 'to the determination of Scripture and Holy Church' and it looked to Henry to 'temper your grace's law accordingly'. As for the demand to submit canon law to Henry's approval, 'we, your most humble subjects, may not submit the execution of our charges and duty, certainly prescribed by God, to your Highness's assent' (Bray, 59). The reply produced the royal reaction which Cromwell had counted on. Henry passed the answer to the speaker of the Commons with a thinly veiled instruction to continue agitation against the church. Then he sent Edward Fox to demand that convocation surrender all claim to legislative independence. When that was resisted he summoned a Commons delegation, denounced the bishops as 'but half our subjects, yea, and scarce our subjects', and, flourishing copies of the incompatible oaths which the bishops took to the king and the pope, sent the MPs away 'to invent some order that we be not thus deluded of our spiritual subjects' (Hall, 788). Faced with the draft of a parliamentary bill which made the clergy 'lower than shoemakers' (*LP Henry VIII*, 5, no. 1013) the church retreated. Henry called off the Commons by proroguing parliament and the upper house of convocation accepted the royal demands in full.

Marriage and the breach with Rome

Thanks in part to the eyewitness account of Edward Hall, the history of what became known as the 'submission of the clergy' provides to later generations a striking vignette of Henry VIII when fully engaged. To contemporaries, it represented the triumph of the radical solution to the Great Matter. The following day Thomas More resigned. Henry's problems could now be settled in England. There followed, however, a strange hesitation. Despite having the enabling legislation ready, parliament was postponed and negotiations at Rome continued. Was Henry concerned about rumbles of aristocratic unhappiness? Was he frustrated by Warham's longevity at Canterbury? Did he need the face-to-face meeting he and Anne had with François I at Calais in October before being able to rely on existing French promises of support? Possibly, but the likeliest explanation is that the king's thinking was not yet free of the chains of convention. The archbishop died at last on 22 August, but when Henry created Anne Boleyn marchioness of Pembroke ten days later, he still thought it wise to provide that the title would descend to her son whether or not born in lawful wedlock. Despite everything, he was not certain that any second marriage while Katherine was alive could be valid.

If Henry was not yet able to break free psychologically, it was very probably Anne who took decisive action. During the visit to Calais or shortly afterwards, she began at long last to sleep with Henry, in all probability following an exchange of vows before witnesses, a procedure which was irregular but nevertheless canonically valid. By the end of the year she could suspect that she was pregnant and in January 1533, probably on the 25th, the two were married—or remarried—in a regular but secret ceremony before dawn in the new Whitehall Palace. Anne was accorded royal status at court from Holy Saturday and given a magnificent coronation seven weeks later. It spread over four days and deliberately manoeuvred the upper classes into endorsing Anne and so showing *hoi polloi* that their betters were fully behind the king's second marriage. Anne gave birth to Princess Elizabeth (later Elizabeth I) on 7 September. There is no doubt that Henry had wanted and expected a boy, but no evidence suggests that the arrival of a girl was the crushing psychological blow which some have supposed. By the following spring Anne was pregnant again and Henry was quite sure that this time it would be a son.

While Henry was at last making public his relationship with Anne, the required formalities were put through by others: Thomas Cromwell, the man whose tactics had undermined the independence of the church, and that other Boleyn protégé, Thomas Cranmer, who was installed as archbishop of Canterbury on 30 March 1533. Parliament passed an Act in Restraint of Appeals which enunciated the *Collectanea* ideology and required ecclesiastical suits to be heard in England. This empowered Cranmer to try the Great Matter and pronounce on 23 May that the marriage with Katherine had been null and void, so making the marriage with Anne fully valid and Princess Mary illegitimate. Katherine of Aragon was reduced to the status of dowager princess of Wales. Rome responded with forceful action at last, condemning the Boleyn match and ordering Henry to take Katherine back. The king responded by formally refusing papal jurisdiction and appealing to a general council of the church, a blatantly schismatic move which implied that the pope was not, under God, the ultimate authority in the church. Further legislation broke all ties with Rome and although Paul III, who succeeded Clement in September 1534, made overtures to win Henry back (which it suited the king to echo), the die had been cast. Henry VIII was 'the only Supreme Head on earth of the Church of England' (Bray, 114).

Establishing the royal supremacy, 1533–1540

Foreign danger

For the remainder of the decade English policy abroad and at home was dominated by the need to defend the supremacy Henry had asserted, and the implications this had for the succession to his throne. The potential for international danger was obvious. Henry's attack on the unity of western Christendom positively challenged the pope to retaliate, while the insult to Katherine and Mary, the emperor's relatives, offered Charles V every incentive to take up the cross on behalf of the holy father. François I had indeed promised Henry some support, but his own agenda was now to win the backing of the newly elected Pope Paul III and to promote the reunion of the western church by a general council, an assembly hardly likely to endorse Henry's claims to supremacy. A papally engineered *rapprochement* between France and the empire would be even more dangerous, facing England with overwhelming odds.

Relations with his 'brother' rulers was very much a king's personal province and initially Henry felt these threats were remote. The pope was restrained by François from declaring Henry deposed. Charles, facing Turkish pressure on his

Habsburg lands in south-eastern Europe and trouble with the German Lutheran princes, showed no wish to add England to his troubles. He confined his protest to words, and blocked the pope's wish to place England under an interdict. Then over the winter of 1535–6 France and the empire came to blows over the duchy of Milan, and the death of Katherine of Aragon on 8 January let Henry announce: 'God be praised that we are free from all suspicion of war now that the real cause of our enmity no longer exists' (*CSP Spain*, 1536–8, 19). The execution of Anne Boleyn which followed in May opened the way to an uncontestable third marriage—to Jane Seymour the same month—and offspring of impeccable legitimacy. In July the king felt strong enough to have convocation rule that no general council of the church could be legal without the consent of all Christian princes—an impossible condition.

At this point the sky began to darken. Following the death of James IV at Flodden, Henry had hoped for friendlier relations with Scotland under its minor heir James V, whose mother was Henry's sister Margaret (1489–1541). However, James refused to break with Rome and in September 1536, with no word to Henry, sailed to France where he married François I's daughter Madeleine on new year's day. Although Madeleine died after a few months, James confirmed his adherence to the 'auld alliance' by a second marriage (June 1538) to Mary of Guise, the daughter of one of François's leading counsellors. In the same month the unthinkable happened. François and Charles accepted papal mediation, ended a war which had brought advantage to neither side, and signed a ten-year truce at Nice. In July the two rulers met at Aigues-Mortes. The pope published the bull deposing Henry and sent agents to both monarchs and to James V pressing for an invasion.

The king of England was less agitated by this diplomatic blizzard than were his ministers. Not only did the emperor have his hands full with a rebellion in Ghent, but Henry knew François and Charles well enough to believe that no reconciliation could last long. Nevertheless, he did take diplomatic measures to counter England's isolation. A peace treaty was signed with Scotland and James V was wooed with gifts. The half-hearted negotiations which Henry had initiated with the Lutheran princes in 1533–4 were revived, and he also made overtures to any state in dispute with Charles or the pope. The king also decided to seek his fourth wife from the anti-imperial camp, and fixed on Anne (1515–1557), the sister of the duke of Cleves, though only after a good deal of wavering. What finalized his decision was possibly Charles's exceptional gesture of trust in François when in the autumn of 1539 he began an imperial progress through France to the Low Countries, with the two monarchs spending Christmas together at Fontainebleau.

Henry backed diplomacy with military preparedness, which continued even after the signs of a split between François and Charles became evident during 1540. As the duke of Suffolk then remarked to Cromwell, 'these bruits be well laid [to rest], but the king does well to provide for the worst' (*LP Henry VIII*, 14/1, no. 749). Henry had inherited a very few ships from his father, but by 1539 he could put over 150 ships to sea including some forty specialized warships. These varied from the *Great Harry*, displacing 1000 tons, to specialized row-barges of 20 tons. Ordnance was revolutionized. Guns had always been one of Henry's enthusiasms—he had set up his own experimental foundry in 1511—and by then had already equipped two of his ships with heavy cannon, firing broadside through gunports, as well as the older lighter pieces mounted on the upper decks. By the time of the crisis, a warship such as the *Mary Rose* might have a broadside of ten heavy guns, many of them now bronze muzzle-loaders, not iron breech-loaders.

Naval preparations were matched by a massive programme of fortifications from the Humber to Milford Haven. Described in 1960 as 'the most extensive scheme of work of its kind undertaken in England until the last or even the present century', the programme exploited the ability of efficient large cannon to inhibit sea-borne landings (O'Neil, 49). Henry again was the driving force. The overall scheme, entitled the 'device by the king' and dating from February 1539 (*LP Henry VIII*, 14/1, no. 398), was drawn up after a survey of 'all the Portes and daungiers on the coastes where any meete or convenient landing place might be supposed', with the king doing part of the inspecting himself (Hall, 828–9). Much of the immediate design was Henry's too. He produced 'plats' and determined details down to the shape of gun embrasures. The resulting style of fortification based on the circular 'gun-tower' has few European counterparts, was short-lived and is frequently dismissed as obsolete in comparison with the angled-bastions of contemporary Italy. However, Henry may have consciously rejected continental models, since a bastion at Camber Castle in the early Italian round form with orillons and attributable to a visiting Moravian 'deviser', was begun and abandoned. Coastal defence did not require buildings to resist a formal siege but protected gun-platforms producing maximum fire power against ships and troops when at the most vulnerable stage of disembarkation.

Domestic enforcement

The external dangers which Henry faced were self-evident. The case was otherwise at home. Henry's claim to the supreme headship introduced England for the first time to the question of conformity in belief. To the age-old requirement to be loyal was added the requirement to think as the king did. Ideology had arrived. Men henceforth would face the choice implicit in Thomas More's last reported words: 'he died the King's good servant but God's first' (Harpsfield, 266). Given the requirements of the common law, measures to enforce the changes domestically and to punish opponents had to be put through parliament, and a comprehensive series of measures was placed on the statute book. The person largely responsible, and now regularly relied on by Henry, was Thomas Cromwell and he also oversaw a nation-wide policy of day-to-day vigilance. A number of instances suggest, however, that Henry was no mere bystander in this, although interested in results rather than method. The king's order, as transmitted by Cromwell, was that 'wheresoever any such cankered malice shall either chance to break out or any to be accused thereof, his highness would have the same tried and thoroughly pursued with great dexterity and as little favour as their demerits shall require' (*LP Henry VIII*, 13/1, no. 107). The king was certainly personally involved in the attempt to force Thomas More to endorse the supremacy, and the parliamentary bill of attainder which in November 1534 followed his obdurate silence. Six months later royal fury at the award of a cardinal's hat to Katherine's champion, Bishop John Fisher, determined Henry to get rid of both this turbulent priest and a former chancellor whose silence shouted from the house-tops. For Henry, convinced beyond reasoning that his status was God given, wilful blindness deserved no mercy.

Alongside legislation went propaganda, derived from the *Collectanea* and the work on papal jurisdiction. The highly successful *A Glasse of Truthe* (1531) was partly the king's own work; intended for a popular audience, it ran to three editions and translations into Latin and French. Henry was present at the council meeting of December 1533 which considered how to promulgate the new ideas and probably authorized publication of *Articles Devised by the Whole Consent of the King's Honourable Council*. It also decided to publish the text of the Act in Restraint of Appeals to Rome in proclamation form to be posted up in market places and the like, and the preambles of other key enactments were used to spread the *Collectanea* ideas. Defenders of the church who had personally felt the king's wrath wrote fulsome retractions, works like Cuthbert Tunstal's *Pro ecclesiasticae unitatis defensione* and Stephen Gardiner's *De vera obedientia*, particularly effective with a clerical readership.

Religious revolution

To contemporaries who, unlike Thomas More, did not appreciate the rationale of the break with Rome, Henry VIII's behaviour appeared schismatic, merely the latest instance of a monarch falling out with a pope. The reality was quite different. Henry had redefined kingship. A supreme headship over the church had been discovered to be integral to the identity of the 'king of England by the grace of God'. All that convocation had done was to recognize fact, and all parliament had done was to provide statutory instruments to enforce the king's God-given personal title. Yet what did it mean for Henry VIII to be head of the church in England?

A common assumption is that Henry maintained orthodoxy except in respect of Rome—the often repeated 'Catholicism without the pope'. Others have argued that he followed a middle course, between traditional religion and reform. However, what neither explanation takes proper account of is the king's determination to take charge and direct the church. In

1535 he appointed Thomas Cromwell to the new post of vicar-general and vicegerent in spirituals and in 1536 injunctions were issued specifying the doctrines to be taught, as well as the way the clergy were to behave and the substantial charitable donations they were to make. What is also not recognized is the extent of the religious change Henry licensed. Certainly this change can often appear inconsistent and erratic, a response to the political realities at home and particularly abroad. For example, during the threats of 1539, Henry gave royal assent to the Act of Six Articles, an apparently draconian statement of orthodoxy. This allowed Cromwell to tell the 1540 parliament that 'the king leaned neither to the right nor to the left' (Lehmberg, *Later Parliaments*, 90). Or again, the king was warned in January 1545 that the imperial alliance he then wanted would be set back unless he checked impending religious changes, so he instructed Cranmer to 'take patience herein and forbear until we espy a more apt and convenient time for the purpose' (*Acts and Monuments*, 5.562). Yet even when external pressures are allowed for, it becomes evident that from the break with Rome onwards, Henry VIII moved progressively towards a personal formulation of Christianity which was as distinct from Rome as it was from Luther.

In making these changes Henry was undoubtedly influenced by those around him. Yet it is important to stress the king's direct input. He worked personally on the antecedents of the Ten Articles of 1536, the first of his definitions of religion, and then instructed Edward Fox to elaborate this into a more substantial statement of faith. When this was issued in 1537 it became known as the Bishops' Book precisely because the king had not had time to vet it, though very soon after publication he sent Cranmer 250 corrections and additions. In 1543 a revision was published, known as the King's Book, with a preface by

Henry in the first person. The final innovation in worship was the King's Primer of 1545 which advanced reform within the externals of tradition, with again a commendatory preface by Henry.

In the story of progressive religious change initiated by Henry, the one doctrinal formulation which may appear to go against the grain is the Six Articles of June 1539. Henry himself drew up the final text, and instead of publishing it like the other formularies of the reign on episcopal or royal authority alone, he chose the form of a penal statute. Certainly the statute's ringing endorsement of transubstantiation and five other traditional doctrines, with dreadful penalties for anyone who denied them, did, as has been suggested, reflect the need to parade orthodoxy at a time when the diplomatic situation was dark and when a rebellion in the north, the Pilgrimage of Grace, had shown how much hostility there was in England to recent religious changes. However, the evident importance Henry attached to the bill (he came down to the Lords himself to ensure that it passed), the vigorous opposition which the bill met from the evangelical bishops (two subsequently resigned), and the reaction of reformers in Europe have convinced most historians that the act was a watershed, a substantive turn by Henry away from the reform of recent years towards conservative reaction.

The problem with this interpretation is that the reformers in the Lords did not question transubstantiation, merely the way Henry himself had chosen to define the real presence; most of their fire was directed at article three, the prohibition on clerical marriage. What is more, when it came to vote, the majority of critics supported the bill. Transubstantiation, indeed, was not the Rubicon between orthodoxy and reform it became in later years. Cranmer and Cromwell did not doubt the miracle of the altar, any more than Anne Boleyn had. Little use was made of the Six Articles Act. When juries of enthusiastic London conservatives seized on the new measure and indicted two (or possibly five) hundred reformers, the king himself intervened. All in all only six people suffered under its provisions. Nor did royal assent to the bill mark the end of reform. During the passage of the measure through parliament, Henry had approved the issuing of the Great Bible, the most significant of his religious reforms, and in 1541 a fine was instituted for parishes which failed to buy a copy. Later that year further feast days were abolished and the order was given to destroy all remaining shrines. The relaxation of the rules for Lent was continued until further notice (an announcement repeated in 1542), and so it went on. Where transubstantiation was important was as a litmus test for Anabaptists, and a more satisfactory explanation for the statute is as the climax of a campaign (no doubt triggered by horror stories of their behaviour in Münster) which since 1535 had seen two proclamations expelling the sect and the burning of over twenty 'twice-baptisers'. The campaign was continued the next year when the advocating of adult baptism and a whole raft of Anabaptist beliefs were excluded from the statutory general pardon, as well as denial of transubstantiation. Henry was not repudiating respectable reformers but religious fanatics.

Significant doctrinal shift (or, as Henry would say, reform) was, of course, implicit in the break with Rome. By claiming that he was rescuing the English church from the evil of papal usurpation, Henry was consciously asserting what had previously been heresy. In its place came Caesaro-papalism, the king as pope in all but name. Henry was the Old Testament King David, come again. Bishops in consequence found themselves holding office during the king's pleasure and being styled 'by royal authority'. As well as this denial of the apostolic succession as it had previously been understood, Henry denied the traditional catholicity of the church. Instead of a visible unity transcending all frontiers and focused on the bishop of Rome as Christ's representative on earth, he understood the church universal to be a metaphysical unity of national churches. Henry never claimed that he was a priest, but he certainly saw himself as the vicar of Christ for England, responsible for what his subjects believed. When he declared in the creed, 'I believe in one Holy Catholic and Apostolic Church' he meant what nobody had meant before.

Henry had no qualms about interfering with belief. True, the king's adamant refusal to countenance justification by faith can suggest strict orthodoxy and so too his adherence to the doctrine of transubstantiation. However, he insisted on each because they were integral to his mechanistic and inadequate understanding of salvation. He did accept the need for faith, but understood this as assent to the creeds, not—as the reformers, Catholic and non-Catholic, understood—a lively personal commitment to God. As for the need for good works, that was equally vital because otherwise there was no incentive to virtue. The supreme good work was the mass, yet what Henry understood the mass to be was distinctly shallow. It was the mechanics of the miracle of transubstantiation which mattered, far more than the mass being the offering of Christ to God. In the will which he drafted in 1544 he described the mass as given 'for our better Remembrance' of the passion of the Lord (Rymer, *Foedera*, 15.110).

Ambiguous on the eucharist, Henry was heretical on the nature of the priesthood. He denied that holy orders were of divine origin and always deleted the adjective when he had the opportunity. He saw no difference between bishops and priests, spoke of the primary function of the clergy as teaching and preaching, and treated them as administrators, not channels of divine grace. Henry also undermined belief in the efficacy of prayers for the dead, a central preoccupation of late medieval western Christendom. His father disposed directly or through his executors of in excess of £50,000 in pious works for the repose of his soul. Henry VIII gave assets worth £600 a year to St George's, Windsor. By 1537 he already accepted that prayers for the dead were only justified by ancient precedent and charity and that their value was only to reduce 'some part' of the pain of the dead of whose condition nothing is known. In 1538 he rejected the word 'purgatory' on the ground that neither purgatory nor the purgation of souls appears in scripture. He did, certainly, take vestigial comfort in knowing that Windsor would pray for him *post mortem*, but his last will is a confused attempt to have it all ways, beseeching the Virgin and saints to pray for:

> Us and with Us whiles We lyve in this World, and in the Time of passing out of the same, so that We may the soner atteyn everlasting Lief after our Departure out of this transitory Lief, which We do both hope and clayme by Christes Passion and Woord. (Rymer, *Foedera*, 15.110)

The King's Primer of 1545 (which Henry claimed as his own) was blunt to a point: 'There is nothing in the dirige [the office of the dead] taken out of scripture that maketh any mention of the souls departed than doth the tale of Robin Hood'.

Henry also made drastic changes in traditional religious practice. From 1536 the clergy were required to preach against superstitious images, relics, miracles, and pilgrimages while injunctions in 1538 ordered the removal of all 'feigned' images and decreed that candles must only be burnt before the rood, the tabernacle (for the host), and the (Easter) sepulchre.

Shrines were destroyed—most notably that of St Thomas at Canterbury—and relics were held up to public ridicule. His promotion of the vernacular Bible defied generations of the English episcopate. In 1543 the king assented to the reform of the service books and in 1545 the King's Primer, in addition to its notable frankness about purgatory, made no mention of the saints. The litany was by then in English (preserving only 5 per cent of the traditional invocations to the saints) and the king had Cranmer working on a communion rite. By the time of Henry's death, Catholic practice had been drastically curtailed. Robert Parkyn, a conservative Yorkshire cleric wrote, 'thus in Kyng Henrie days began holly churche in Englande to be in greatt ruyne as it appearide daly' (Dickens, 295).

The most evident of Henry VIII's destructions was the ruin of English monasticism. That there was a need for reform was widely agreed. Every king for more than a century had dissolved religious houses and applied the income to charitable purposes thought more relevant, and a strong body of opinion now saw the opportunity for a major redistribution of monastic wealth into education and charity. On the other hand, given that the total income of religious houses equalled or even exceeded that of the crown, the temptation to secularize the wealth of the monasteries was dazzling. In 1533, as the Act in Restraint of Appeals to Rome was passing through the Commons, Henry was already talking of reuniting 'to the crown the goods which Churchmen held of it, which his predecessors could not alienate to his prejudice' (*LP Henry VIII*, 6, no. 235). In the end the argument for immediate limited secularization prevailed, but without commitment for the future, and in 1536 about 250 of the smaller religious houses were dissolved by act of parliament, bringing the crown in excess of £70,000 gross over the next thirty months. Subsequently the greater houses fell in to the crown, generally by surrender; the last, Waltham Abbey, did so in April 1540. The detail of all this was handled by Thomas Cromwell, but there is no doubt that secularization was fully supported by Henry. Indeed, he may have appeared in the Commons in person to promote the 1536 Dissolution Bill and in 1543 he specifically condemned 'the superstitious works of men's own invention...in which...them that were lately called religious (as monks, friars, nuns, and such other), have in times past put their great trust and confidence' (Lacey, 158).

Opposition and the Pilgrimage of Grace

For Henry VIII, recovering royal supremacy over the church and exploiting it to produce reform was the achievement of his reign. Beneath the great family portrait which Holbein painted for the wall of the privy chamber in Whitehall Palace was the assertion that Henry:

> drives the unworthy from the altars and brings in men of integrity. The presumption of popes has yielded to unerring virtue and with Henry VIII bearing the sceptre in his hand, religion has been restored and with him on the throne the truths of God have begun to be held in due reverence. (Strong, 57, trans. E. W. Ives and C. R. Ives)

Yet the more the extent of Henry's Reformation is appreciated, the more difficult it becomes to account for the limited reaction which it produced. To a degree this can be explained by Henry moving progressively and spasmodically. He had no initial agenda beyond vindicating his kingly identity, but the logic of Caesaro-papalism drove towards heterodoxy. It is also true that engrained loyalty to the crown was a huge disincentive to protest. Nevertheless, the populous south of England rebelled against excessive taxation, and its failure to rise in support of

the traditional church suggests that the changes Henry introduced were greeted with enough support or apathy to disable
concerted challenge. It is noteworthy that the latter part of his
reign saw a spontaneous reduction in provision for prayers for
the dead as endowed chantries were voluntarily surrendered in
large numbers.

The partial exception to the picture of acquiescence, whether
grudging or positive, was the country north of the Wash. On
1 October 1536 the county of Lincoln broke out in unrest,
followed a week later by large areas of Yorkshire and beyond.
The Lincolnshire rising lasted about a fortnight, but nine well-
armed and organized 'hosts', numbering 30,000 in all, retained
control of the northern counties for several months. Henry VIII
called the protesters 'rebels' but they saw themselves acting 'for
the commonwealth' on a 'pilgrimage for grace' from the king,
and their object was:

> the preservacyon of Crystes churche, of thys realme of Eng-
> land, the kynge our soverayne lord, the nobylytie and comyns
> of the same, and to the entent to macke petycion to the
> kynges highnes for the reformacyon of that whyche is amysse
> within thys realme and for the punnyshement of the hery-
> tykes and subverters of the lawes. (Dodds and Dodds, 1.176)

Although this manifesto indicates a complex of general discon-
tents, there can be little doubt that religion was the catalyst, not
only the start of monastic dissolution but a sense of threat to the
church overall. The pilgrims marched under the banner of the
five wounds of Christ and the banner of St Cuthbert.

Henry's response to the Lincolnshire rising was to bluster and
to threaten, but the Tudor system of support for the civil power
worked well. Several noblemen put their retainers in readiness,

so providing the king with a force in short order, and this was sufficient to persuade the gentlemen of the county that it was better to represent their own involvement as a responsible attempt to prevent violence and to let a leaderless peasantry slink home. Forty-six executions followed. The Pilgrimage of Grace was a different order of problem and caught the king out badly. He had disbanded the forces gathered for Lincolnshire and the principal reason the situation did not get worse was because the pilgrims had no intention of marching south. New royal forces which had to be raised arrived piecemeal and were hopelessly outnumbered, thus forcing the duke of Norfolk to parley. However, as he wrote to the king, 'I beseche you to take in gode part what so ever promes I shall make unto the rebells, for sewerly I shall observe no part thereof' (Dodds and Dodds, 1.260). A truce followed, during which Henry continued to insist that he would punish Robert Aske, the captain of the pilgrims and the other ringleaders, but eventually he had to concede a general pardon and the promise of a parliament. Before the pilgrims agreed to disband, Norfolk was forced to agree in addition that the abbeys should be restored until the parliament met, but he was able to avoid promising a further dangerous concession which Henry was prepared to make, that parliament should meet wherever they wished it.

The king's next move was not what the trusting northerners expected. He had been outmanoeuvred in the field, but not in guile. He never had any intention of honouring promises made, and so remained silent, though he did get Norfolk to woo the gentry. Sir Francis Bigod of Settrington in the East Riding, a former MP, realized the king's dishonesty and called out the East Riding men in January, but he was unpopular with his neighbours, had no gentry backing, and the rising collapsed. The next month the commoners of Cumberland decided to go it alone, only to be defeated in an attack on Carlisle. These outbreaks of disorder were what Henry had been counting on to provide the excuse to wipe out in blood the disgrace of his surrender. The gentry leaders were rounded up for trial and Norfolk declared martial law on the north. Henry's endorsement was enthusiastic:

> You shal in any wise cause suche dredfull execution to be doon upon a good nombre of thinhabitauntes of every towne, village and hamlet that have offended in this rebellion, aswell by hanging of them uppe in trees, as by the quartering of them and the setting of their heddes and quarters in every towne, greate and small, and in al suche other places as they may be a ferefull spectacle to all other herafter that wold practise any like matter whiche we requyre you to doo, without pitie or respecte. (*State Papers, Henry VIII*, 2.538)

In all upwards of 200 died. The 1536 risings were contained geographically because of the loyalty to the crown of the majority of the nobility of the south and the midlands, and the willingness of the servants, tenants, and 'well-wishers' who comprised their 'powers', to side with them. This was true even of the group of supporters erstwhile of Katherine of Aragon, now of Princess Mary, who were fully in sympathy with the aims of the northerners. The most notable, Henry Courtenay, marquess of Exeter, was the king's cousin, had been brought up by Henry, and served in the privy chamber staff; Lord Montagu and Sir Geoffrey Pole were sons of Margaret Pole, countess of Salisbury, the king's cousin once removed. Yet their loyalty was palpably grudging. Unwilling to challenge Henry's changes but also unwilling to accept them, Exeter and the Poles continued to use their standing at court to express criticism. Their support for Katherine and Mary had significantly alienated Henry, but he became paranoiac over the behaviour of Margaret's other son, the cleric Reginald Pole, whose education he had also fostered. In 1536, from the safety of the continent, Reginald addressed a swingeing public criticism of his former patron:

> You have squandered a huge treasure; you have made a laughing-stock of the nobility; you have never loved the people; you have pestered and robbed the clergy in every possible way; and lately you have destroyed the best men in your kingdom [Fisher and More], not like a human being, but like a wild beast. (Schenk, 71)

Pole was then created a cardinal and sent to Flanders in February 1537 to try to implement the bull excommunicating the king. Henry replied by vowing the destruction of the Poles. Geoffrey was forced to provide evidence of treasonable intent against his brother and Exeter, who were executed in January 1539 along with Montagu's brother-in-law Sir Edward Neville, a long-serving gentleman of the privy chamber; a gentleman of even longer service, Sir Nicholas Carew, followed in March 1539. Exeter's wife and son and Montagu's son were incarcerated in the Tower along with the countess of Salisbury; the countess was beheaded in May 1541, leaving Reginald and his disgraced brother Geoffrey as the sole survivors of the blood royal outside the immediate Tudor family.

Henry VIII: the man

The character of the king

The greatest challenge to Henry VIII's rule was the risings of 1536—indeed they were the largest peacetime revolt in English history. His response is very revealing of his attitude to kingship. Egoism dominated. This may be understandable in the case of the Great Matter, but for Henry, the right to rule was innate and uncircumscribed. His response to the Lincolnshire protesters had been abuse:

> How presumptuous then are ye, the rude commons of one shire, and that one of the most brute and beastly of the whole realm, and of least experience, to find fault with your prince ... whom ye are bound by all laws to obey and serve, with both your lives, lands and goods, and for no worldly cause to withstand.

He had demanded one hundred selected scapegoats (*LP Henry VIII*, 11, no. 780(2)). And this response Henry described as 'conceived as of itself to make them repent their follies and ask mercy without any tarrying!' (ibid., no. 780(1)). Nor was this uncharacteristic. When he discovered that the council had written to France on his accession offering amity and peace (that is, the continuation of his father's policy) he burst out: 'Who wrote this letter? I ask peace of the King of France who dares not look me in the face, still less make war on me?' (*CSP Venice, 1509–19*, 11). A month before his death he rejected requests to include Stephen Gardiner among the council for the next reign saying: 'You should never rule him, he is of so troublesome a nature. Marry . . . , I myself could use him and rule him to all manner of purposes, as seemed good unto me; but so shall you never do' (*Acts and Monuments*, 5.691–2). Henry's rooted conviction was that he possessed superior wisdom and that it was unforgivable presumption to challenge him, an impertinence towards the Lord's anointed which was conclusive evidence of fixed malevolence. The vindictiveness he displayed in the aftermath of the Pilgrimage was duplicated in the attack on the Scots in 1544, when he ordered men, women, and children in and around Edinburgh to be put to fire and sword for Scottish 'falsehood and disloyalty' (Bain, 2.326).

Egoism was compounded by falsity and deceit. During the Pilgrimage of Grace the king invited Robert Aske to meet him secretly 'to here of your mouthe the hole circumstance and begynning of that matier' (*State Papers, Henry VIII*, 2.523) and he later wrote to thank him for his efforts to calm the north. The erstwhile captain of the pilgrims was then tricked into returning to London so that the king could 'wade with him with fair words as though he had great trust in him' and once that disguised interrogation was over, arrest him (*LP Henry VIII*, 12/1, no. 698(1)). Henry was very much the *faux bonhomme*; after Thomas More had been seen walking with the royal arm round his shoulders, the future martyr commented that the king would behead him without a qualm if it 'could win him a castle in France' (Roper, ed. Hitchcock, 21). Indeed to free Henry to invade France, Edmund de la Pole, Edward IV's nephew, had been beheaded in 1513, despite assurances which Henry VII had given that he would be spared. Henry VIII executed more English notables than any other monarch before or since. The victims comprised two wives, one cardinal, over twenty members of peerage families, four prominent public servants, and six of the king's close attendants and friends. And this takes no account of the three mitred abbots and various heads of major monastic houses who were executed, nor of Cardinal Wolsey and the three members of aristocratic stock who died in prison or on the way there. As Thomas Wyatt wrote, 'circa Regna tonat' ('round the throne the thunder rolls'; Wyatt, 185).

Linked to this was the king's ability to deny reality, an obstinate conviction that facts were as he understood or wanted to understand them and not as they were. Among armchair strategists Henry had few equals. At the height of the Pilgrimage he wrote to the embattled Norfolk:

> it is moche to our mervayl to receyve soo many desperate letters from yow, and in the same no remedyes. We might thinke that either thinges be not so wel loked on as they might bee, whenne youe canne loke but only to thone side, or elles that youe be soo perplexed with the brutes of the oon parte that ye doo omytt to write the good of thother. (*State Papers, Henry VIII*, 2.517)

This refusal to face facts could at times lead to remarkable political blindness. Henry knew he depended on 'men of power and worship' and during his reign steadily built up the number of important landowners who were sworn to his service. Yet when Norfolk was at his wit's end to find the men of the substance and reputation vital to restore normality to areas which had supported the Pilgrimage, Henry responded in his own handwriting: 'We woll not be bound of a necessitie to be served with lordes. But we woll be served with such menn of what degree soever as we shall appoint to the same' (*LP Henry VIII*, 12/1, no. 636).

Egoistical self-righteousness made Henry both the most forgiving and the most unforgiving of men. An alleged offender who could reach him in person, abjectly confess himself guilty of what the king suspected, whether true or not, and throw himself on royal mercy, would in so doing confirm Henry's perspicacity and could expect mercy. As the king is reported to have said after Stephen Gardiner had confessed to popish leanings, 'you know what my nature and custom hath been in such matters, evermore to pardon them that will not dissemble, but confess their fault' (*Acts and Monuments*, 5.690). On the other hand, if the king detected dissembling, 'stiffness', or ingratitude he would be brutal and harsh in the extreme, as the attack on Courtenay and the Poles demonstrates.

The French ambassador Charles de Marillac identified other traits. Writing to the duc de Montmorency in 1540 he pointed to three major vices. 'The first is that he is so covetous that all the riches in the world would not satisfy him'. The second was suspicion and fear so that 'he dares not trust a single man', and the third 'lightness and inconstancy' (*LP Henry VIII*, 15, no. 954). Henry's passion for money is well attested and supremely seen in the rape of the church, not only the secularization of the monasteries but the start of 'voluntary' land exchanges with the bishops. As for unpredictability and suspicion (for which he was notorious) Henry represented this as policy: 'if I thought that my cap knew my counsel, I would cast it into the fire and burn it' (Cavendish, 184). Some scholars accept this as evidence of the king's decisiveness and independence. For them Henry is an authoritative individual determining the conduct of affairs. Nothing got by him and he behaved as he wished, when he wished. The alternative view is that the mistrust and the variability reflected a fundamental insecurity. Later generations have known Henry overwhelmingly through the paintings of Hans Holbein the younger but this image of the dominant hero was the creation of the artist. Earlier likenesses of Henry VIII suggest nothing of the kind. Precisely why Henry suffered from insecurity can only be conjectured. Perhaps he learned watchfulness and extreme caution from his father, and his continued failure to have a male heir meant that until middle age he was always vulnerable as the sole male Tudor. However, his son's birth in 1537 only switched anxiety to the boy. Henry's habits of mind were fixed and his sense of insecurity reached its peak in the last decade of the reign.

Vulnerability

How did Henry VIII's approach to kingship affect politics? His personality was certainly determinative, as must be the case with any single individual heading a pyramid of power. Furthermore, in any such power structure, gaining and keeping the confidence of the head is crucial to success, with the result that the organic form of interaction is faction and a competition for favour and reward. Those scholars who see Henry in the Holbein mould, strong and confident, argue that he exploited faction within the royal entourage to his own advantage, in particular to free himself from dependence on any group or individual and make himself the lodestar of officials and courtiers. Against this, scholars who see the public persona as a mask for inner uncertainty argue that the king was vulnerable to persuasion and that factions set out to influence the king's mind on both matters of patronage and of policy.

The pressure on Henry to abandon Wolsey and the king's reluctance to do so certainly indicate that on that occasion the king was responding, not leading. The radical solution to his matrimonial dilemma was similarly sold to him in the teeth of traditionalists who advised otherwise. In both cases Anne Boleyn was central, and on her and the influence she could wield focused all those who supported change, not only the royal supremacy but the more evangelical stance in religion which she represented. Moderate reform progressed in the 1530s because initially Anne and subsequently Cranmer and Cromwell had command of the king's ear. Anne Boleyn patronized and promoted clergy of a reforming turn of mind. Cromwell was a convinced reformer—he even lost money on the printing of the Great Bible. Cranmer, who had an intimacy with Henry which nothing could shake, moved steadily towards doctrinal change. As John Foxe wrote: 'so long as Queen Anne, Thomas Cromwell, Archbishop Cranmer, Master Denny, Doctor Butts with such like were about him and could prevail with him, what organ of Christ's glory did more good in the church than he [Henry VIII]?' (*Acts and Monuments*, 5.605). There is no incompatibility between a Henry whose will was law and a Henry who was capable of being influenced. Indeed his suspicious nature precisely exposed him to suggestion. Wolsey said: 'be well advysed and assured what matter ye put in his hed, for ye shall neuer pull it owt agayn' (Cavendish, 179).

Husband and father

Henry VIII of course did not leave egoism, pig-headedness, and distrust behind when he entered his private apartments.

Evidence about his relations with his first wife, Katherine of Aragon, is sparse. Initially Henry behaved as the perfect courtly lover, but the suspicion is that once more egoism was the real motive. Katherine was a beautiful object, an audience for his chivalric posturing. In the early years—while her international connections were useful—he appears to have relied on her for help and advice in diplomacy, and she was an effective 'governor of the realm' during the first French war. How intimate their relation was is another matter. In 1511 he held a tournament in honour of his wife on the birth of their first son, only for the child to die a week later. Undoubtedly Henry was disappointed, but his response was to go in for a bout of gambling and then to order another tournament, action which certainly does not suggest real closeness between him and his sorrowing wife. There are a few stories and hints of extra-marital flirtations. For example Jeanne Poppingcourt, a Frenchwoman in Katherine's household, had a lively reputation and Henry gave her £100 on her return to France in 1516. However the king's only definite liaisons during the Aragon marriage were with Elizabeth Blount and Mary Carey, *née* Boleyn. Elizabeth was one of the queen's ladies, cousin to her chamberlain. The *affaire* with her, which gave Henry his only known bastard child, possibly began in 1518 and may have lasted as little as a year. The relationship with Mary Carey is known only by Henry's own admission years later (there were no acknowledged children) but it must have taken place in the early 1520s. By the standards of contemporary popes and monarchs that record was sexually modest, but scholars differ as to the reason. Was it fidelity, morality, or lack of interest? Another possibility is increasing anxiety, possibly leading to impotence, the consequence of his inability to produce offspring which survived. In the 1530s he was certainly having psychosexual problems.

Henry's relationship with Anne Boleyn began, as already noted, in 1526. At first a typically selfish effort by Henry to possess the most exciting woman at court, it soon turned into genuine passion, what Henry called his 'so-great folly' (Savage, 30). However, his decision to substitute a love match for the intended liaison with Anne led Henry into uncharted waters, to a royal marriage based on emotion, in place of the norm of an arranged union with a foreign princess based on diplomatic advantage. The result was almost unique in royal circles, a story of sunshine and storm in which a feisty Anne alternately entranced and infuriated a besotted Henry. Anne, however, also exerted real influence. Her positive input during the divorce crisis continued, not only in the promotion of evangelical change but in patronage issues, in exploiting her French connections for diplomatic advantage, and as the leader of the predominant faction at court.

The unique closeness between Henry and Anne throughout their marriage gives the lie to the popular belief that the king rapidly tired of this second wife and hence had her arrested on Tuesday 2 May 1536. True, to Henry's great distress, the queen (who had miscarried in the summer of 1534) miscarried again on 29 January 1536. Fanciful explanations for Anne's rejection have been built on the supposition that the foetus on this occasion was deformed. They are completely without foundation. The story about deformity appeared in Roman Catholic black propaganda some fifty years after Anne's death along with the claim that Anne was Henry's daughter! The 1536 miscarriage was, nevertheless, important because it stirred Henry's doubts, not about Anne, but about God. God had not permitted him sons by Katherine. Was he frowning on this marriage too? Henry was also suffering from the aftermath of a crashing fall in the tiltyard five days earlier which left

him unconscious for two hours. With Anne out of circula-tion after childbirth, the traditionalist faction at court allied with the king's new protégé, Edward Seymour, to organize a claque against Anne and entice Henry with the milk and water charms of Edward's sister Jane (1508/9–1537). Yet as long as the king continued firmly committed to his marriage to Anne, all this was mere dalliance, and only a fortnight before she was arrested Henry was going to great lengths to force the representative of Charles V to recognize her as his queen.

The campaign of the conservative faction became dangerous only when it was joined by Thomas Cromwell. Hitherto he had been Anne's faithful supporter, but in late March they fell out, principally over the decision to secularize rather than redirect the assets of the smaller monasteries. Anne's attempt to block secularization failed, but it had resulted in a very public breach with the minister, and he knew that no more than Wolsey could he survive for long with Anne as his enemy. Cromwell therefore made peace with the traditionalist faction at court and left them to dangle the bait of Jane Seymour. He mean-while misrepresented the liveliness of the queen's admirers as evidence of sexual misconduct by Anne and the leading mem-bers of her faction (particularly Henry Norris, groom of the stool), and used that to provoke the king's suspicions. Henry, taken unawares, challenged Norris (the nearest he had to a friend), offering pardon if he would confess his offence. Norris refused to lie in order to save his neck and went to the block along with Anne's brother and some smaller fry, and in the afternoon of the same day Cranmer declared her marriage was null and void. The justification seems to have been that, though not realized previously, Henry's relationship with Anne, after having relations with her sister, broke God's law in the same

way as his relationship with Katherine of Aragon after her 'alleged' intercourse with Prince Arthur. With Henry now at peace with the Almighty, Anne was executed on 19 May. His only gesture to Anne was the 'kindness' of a French headsman to execute her in the continental fashion. Henry married Jane eleven days later.

Henry's seventeen-month marriage to Jane Seymour was too short to leave traces of much influence. The memory of Anne was never far away and when Jane pleaded for the abbeys during the Pilgrimage, Henry reminded her 'that the last queen had died in consequence of meddling too much with state affairs' (*LP Henry VIII*, 11, no. 1250). However, the motto Jane adopted—'Bound to obey and serve'—suggests that she understood this very well and styled herself in deliberate contrast to her predecessor. Colourless she may appear, but Jane Seymour achieved something which neither Katherine nor Anne had managed, a healthy male child who grew to adolescence. Henry was genuinely broken when his wife died twelve days after the birth and to his death Henry represented Jane as his 'true and loving wife' (Rymer, *Foedera*, 15.111). It is, however, impossible to evaluate this emotion; was it deep personal bereavement or regret at the loss of the first partner whose marriage was undeniably valid and had been endorsed by God giving the son he had withheld for so long?

The birth of Edward (later Edward VI) in September 1537 settled the final shape of the king's family—Henry's bastard son, the duke of Richmond, had died in July 1536. In the fashion of the time, Henry, not the mother, took responsibility for care and upbringing—in Edward's case he wrote out the regimen in his own hand. However, against the fashion of the time Henry displayed real fondness for his infant offspring, willing to spend a considerable time playing with them. At appropriate ages they were each given a separate household and arrangements made for an excellent education. Children were also valuable pieces on the chessboard of European diplomacy and Henry exploited the possibility of making marriages for them from an early age. Mary was betrothed at the age of two, Elizabeth's marriage was under discussion before her first birthday, and Edward's marriage—the greatest prize—was fixed when he was five and a half.

As the children grew, their relationship with their father changed. He expected absolute obedience and deference and their letters to him display 'half fearful delight'. The turmoil of his first two marriages had, of course, a major impact on his daughters. When Elizabeth was declared illegitimate by the second Succession Act of July 1536, the precocious $2\frac{1}{2}$-year-old noticed the change—'how hap it yesterday Lady Princess and today but Lady Elizabeth'. Indeed, the king had to be reminded to provide for her (*Rutland MSS*, 1.310). Nevertheless, her age and the fact that her attendants remained unchanged cushioned the impact of her mother's death and her change of fortune. Not so her elder sister. Mary experienced what can only be described as long-term parental abuse which probably accounts for some of her later obsessions and possibly for her recurrent ill health. By 1531, when she was sixteen, she had become a bone of contention between her parents and when, following her mother's reduction to the rank of princess dowager in the summer of 1533, Mary insisted on still being styled 'Princess', Henry closed her establishment and sent her to reside as the poor relation of the new heir, Elizabeth. Mary behaved impossibly and rejected Anne Boleyn's overtures with insult, but it has been suggested that Henry was not so much angry with his daughter as jealous of her relationship with Katherine. He allowed her to see Mary only once more. What is certainly true is that he was determined to enforce obedience to his will.

That determination produced a second political crisis in 1536. Following the fall of Anne Boleyn, Mary, and her traditionalist allies at court, had expected that, with 'that woman' out of the way, she would be restored to favour and recognized as heir presumptive. Cromwell, however, knew better and exploited his certainty that Henry was determined that Mary should first admit her illegitimacy. The father put intense psychological pressure on his daughter, and a number of her supporters were either sent to the Tower or interrogated. Faced with the choice between her own integrity and their liberty—and perhaps lives—Mary cracked, and admitted that her parents had never been legally married. A month later the second Succession Act declared that, like Elizabeth, she too was a bastard. Mary's surrender saved her friends, but, as Cromwell had calculated, he was now free of his erstwhile traditionalist allies. The cost to the princess was incalculable.

With his elder daughter returned, as Henry saw it, to proper filial obedience, the family settled to a kind of normality. Only Katherine Parr (1512–1548) of his later wives had much of an impact, particularly in respect of Elizabeth and Edward. The most important consideration in this final decade was the king's increasing age and ill health. Henry was putting on an enormous amount of weight: his chest measurement reached 57 inches and his waist 54 and eventually he had to be moved around his palaces in a 'trauewe', a sort of carrying chair. He also suffered enormous pain from a chronic leg ulcer which produced dangerous attacks of fever. The cause was not syphilis (voluminous medical evidence proves that his doctors never treated him for this well-recognized condition) but either varicose veins or osteomyelitis, and the ulcer was made much worse by Henry's insistence on riding. He could become black in the face with pain.

The realm reshaped

Henry VIII and Thomas Cromwell

Henry VIII owed the successful assertion of his royal supremacy to the political skills of Thomas Cromwell. It is, however, more difficult to separate king and minister in the secular affairs of the 1530s. One of the most important developments concerned parliament. In the first place it was called more frequently. From 1509 to 1531 there were eleven sessions; from 1532 to 1540 there were ten. More than that, the legislation after 1532 asserted the novel competence of statute to enforce the religious authority of the supreme head of the church and the ability of parliament to override property rights, most notably in the dissolution of the monasteries. Government departments were created from scratch. Law reform became a frequent item, accelerating after 1540 and signalling a shift from change achieved by judicial construction to make change by legislative enactment. The succession to the crown was registered. In all, the last twelve parliamentary sessions of Henry's reign, average duration ten weeks, produced upwards of 500 bills which received the royal assent and many others which did not.

This growth of parliament's authority, capacity, and legislative output in no way trenched on the standing of the monarchy. Royal supremacy over the church was implemented through, not granted by, parliament, and was not in conflict with a headship inherent in Henry's person. In 1542 he declared 'we, at no time stand so highly in our estate royal as in the time of parliament, wherein we as head and you as members are conjoined and knit together into one body politic' (Elton, 277). Parliament was the supreme expression of kingly power, and Henry treated it as such. He was meticulous in monitoring and managing the two houses either through Cromwell and his fellow counsellors or, if need be, by his personal appearances. The Commons was not 'packed' but from 1529 the king added fourteen English borough seats in part to facilitate the attendance of men he wanted in the lower chamber. The crown also took care to manage by-elections (a requirement of lengthier parliaments) and to advise unhelpful peers to stay away. Once parliament was in session the king never allowed himself to be far away from Westminster. Henry also used parliament as a forum through which to address the political nation. The most famous instance was in 1545 when he wept when commenting on the lack of charity which religious dissension was producing between those 'to styff in the old Mumpsimus' and those 'to busy and curious in their new Sumpsimus' (Hall, 866).

The historian A. F. Pollard argued that by using parliament to effect the Reformation, Henry took the nation into partnership. A more realistic comment would be that whatever the king claimed or wanted, only parliament could provide teeth sharp enough to enforce his will. It was essentially a tool of royal power. This is amply demonstrated in the treason legislation which gave Henry's reign such a bloody harvest. The treason statute of 1352 he inherited covered only an overt attempt to kill or dethrone the prince. From 1531 to 1544 twelve statutes enacted that a spectrum of offences were high treason. The most notorious, passed in 1534, 'made words treason' but in fact only expressed in statute what was already judge-made law. However the others ranged from the protection against criticism of Henry's various marriages (including criticism in print) to punishing mass poisoning, forging the king's privy seal, signet, or sign manual, and refusing to swear the oath renouncing papal authority.

Pollard also saw Henry VIII as the great architect of parliament. On occasion the king's initiative is beyond doubt. The refusal of the Commons to accept the compromise on the subject of uses which he had offered in 1532 convinced Henry that the MPs deserved no mercy. He exploited his influence in the law courts to win a test case in 1535 which undermined all property titles based on a use. Disaster thus faced landowners, but instead of compromise Henry now insisted that the 1536 session grant him his full pound of flesh. The social disruption which followed figured among the grievances of the Lincolnshire and Yorkshire rebels. In the second session of 1536 he retrospectively justified the Boleyn divorce by a general enactment that relationships of consanguinity and affinity were created not only by marriage but also by illicit sexual intercourse. His last-minute discovery that the duke of Norfolk's half-brother had contracted himself to marry his niece, led to an act of attainder being rushed through all stages on the final morning of that same session, along with a general enactment that marrying into the royal family without permission was a treasonable offence. In 1542 a clause was attached to the act of attainder against Katherine Howard (1518x24–1542) which declared that any unchaste woman who married the king was a traitor.

On the other hand, it has been vigorously argued that in general, policy originated more with Thomas Cromwell than with Henry. There can be no doubt that as well as being principally responsible for the drafting and the passage of legislation, the minister provided the initiative in many measures. He clearly always had a preference for statute as an instrument of government where Henry's instinct was to stand on prerogative. Cromwell must be credited with the legislation which provided administrative machinery to deal with church wealth (the provision for a treasurer and general receiver of first fruits and tenths in 1534 and the court of augmentations in 1536) as well as the 1539 Statute of Proclamations which provided him as vicegerent with better ways to enforce religious change. He was, too, almost certainly behind the large number of statutes which addressed social and economic problems. The first 1536 session, for example, legislated on fishing, leather, horses, pirates, enclosures, cloth manufacture, maximum prices, harbours, and town improvement, issues hardly likely to have been proposed by Henry any more than the 1536 poor-law statute which can certainly be credited to Cromwell. Indeed, thanks to the comprehensiveness of Cromwellian legislation directed to 'the common weal', parliament became for Englishmen the accepted mechanism through which desired change, nationally, locally, and individually, could be achieved.

But all this said, Henry VIII was certainly more involved in government in the 1530s and after than during Wolsey's ministry. Cromwell's own briefing notes for his meetings with the king show how careful the minister was to keep him informed even on the most minor matters. It is, therefore, best to see Henry recreating with Cromwell the chairman–managing director relationship which he had had with the cardinal, although from time to time having a more direct input. Nevertheless, overall, he still more often sanctioned government action than initiated it.

Wales, Calais, and the north

Thanks to the authority of parliament, significant changes were made in the structure of Henry's dominions. The first to 'benefit' was Wales. In 1509 the principality consisted of some forty-five quasi-independent marcher lordships, the legacy of the piecemeal conquest of earlier centuries, plus the six coastal counties set up by Edward I. The chronic problem was lawlessness since the crown had very little authority in either counties or lordships, and effective power was in local hands. A council in the marches of Wales had existed under different guises off and on since 1476, but to limited effect, even after Wolsey strengthened its authority and machinery in 1525 when Princess Mary was sent to Ludlow as its nominal head. There were no better results from the other measures periodically tried by Henry VII and Henry himself: aggregating local offices in the hands of a royal nominee to create an artificial 'proconsul', or imposing indentures on the marcher lords. In January 1534 a final attempt at discipline began with the appointment of Rowland Lee, a Cromwell protégé, as bishop of Chester (that is, Coventry and Lichfield) and as president of the council in the marches, a man 'stowte of nature, redie witted, roughe in speeche, not affable to any of the Walshrie, an extreme severe ponisher of offenders, desirous to gayne credit with the king and comendacion for his service' (Williams, 82). The appointment was followed at the autumn session of parliament by legislation which, *inter alia*, gave marcher lords a financial interest in doing justice, placed their officers under the supervision of the council, and allowed prosecution for lawlessness in Wales to take place in the nearest English shire.

Two years later there was a remarkable volte-face. Bills were put into parliament to integrate Wales and England, introduce English law and institutions into the principality, and divide it into counties on the English model with twenty-seven MPs, a policy completed by a statute of 1543. A further act of 1536 abolished local franchises and rights of jurisdiction in England. In the same session, too, the government of Calais was dealt with comprehensively in the lengthiest of all Henrician enactments, which included granting it two seats in parliament like any English borough. Taken together, this 1536 legislation can be seen as powerful evidence of a deliberate crown policy to move towards a sovereign unitary state. Moreover, since these moves substantially coincide with Cromwell's period as chief minister and are congruent with the legislation he carried through asserting national independence against the pope, with the preambles to statutes which he drafted, the policies advocated by writers in his employ, and the language of his own letters, it is obvious to allow him much of the credit.

On the other hand there must be real doubts about the depth of the king's interest in the Cromwellian agenda. He undoubtedly endorsed anything which expressed what he saw as proper to his authority, but Henry himself appears to have been motivated more by pragmatism than ideas. For example, in Wales he had been personally involved in preparing the 1534 legislation and early in 1536 he asked Rowland Lee to devise 'further articles for the helping of Wales' (*LP Henry VIII*, 10, no. 330). However, Lee was given no inkling of any intended shift to a policy of integration and it was a month into the parliament before news of the U-turn reached him—to his utter horror. The 1536 act was also drafted with a provision for the king to suspend it which had to be invoked in the following February. Two years later matters were still held up and the crown admitted that the reorganization of Wales had run into trouble because the king had been too busy. All this suggests that the act was introduced with inadequate forethought and smacks very much of an impulsive change of mind by Henry. Admittedly, in requesting Cromwell to 'considre and kepe the fomer statutes provided for the saide Countreye of Wales' Lee could be implying that the legislation was down to the minister, but the news which had reached him was that 'the Kinges Graces pleasure was to make Wales Shiregrounde' (*State Papers, Henry VIII*, 1.454–5).

Similarly, the source of the interest which eventually produced the Calais legislation of 1536 was an inspection of the town which the king made in person during his visit in 1532. He then produced a comprehensive 'Devyse' for remodelling the defences according to his own interpretation of modern warfare, but when after two and a half years little had been done, Henry ordered William Fitzwilliam and the duke of Norfolk to survey the defences again as they visited Calais on embassy. Their report led to a special commission of inquiry being sent out in the autumn of 1535, headed by Fitzwilliam, which 'founde this towne and marches farre out of order' and in part needing to be remedied by an act of parliament (Lehmberg, *Reformation Parliament*, 239).

Pragmatism rather than principles certainly determined the degree of royal interest in Calais at other times during Henry's reign. Holding the town was important to all English kings, and especially to Henry, because it proclaimed the right to the French crown and provided a ready base for intervening on the continent. On the other hand, of itself, Calais was a municipality in economic decline and with a falling English population, a fortified town with a poor harbour, built in a drained marsh in defiance of nature. Its strength lay in its water defences, but as Wolsey was told in 1527, 'watyr works be straunge & mervelus to kepe in ordyr but yff they may be contynually oversene & also holpyn in tyme' (*History of the King's Works*, 3.344). However, instead of a steady investment in maintenance and repair, the policy was one of emergency patching-up. Action was forthcoming only when external circumstances drew attention to the town.

In 1512 the declaration of war with France had been accompanied by a ruling that the offspring of the increasing number of mixed marriages in Calais should henceforth be counted as English. The Calais conferences of 1520 and 1522 were followed by the release of considerable sums for repairs and fortifications. In 1527 Wolsey inspected the evidence of major sea damage, after which the sea wall was replaced and the king issued proclamations ordering the town to be repaired and offering customs privileges in the hope of revived trading at Calais (and hence the funds available). After the 1536 act Calais again went on the back burner but the diplomatic crisis of 1539 gave it the highest priority and the resulting modernization produced, as Norfolk boasted, 'the strongest town in Christendom' (*LP Henry VIII*, 16, no. 850). The three outer defences of Calais—at Newneham Bridge, Guînes, and Hammes—were also updated and six new 'bulwarks' were built. The overall cost of the fortification programme between 1538 and 1547 was £120,700.

Pragmatic considerations rather than grand theory may also account for the statute of 1536 abolishing palatinates and franchises. The principal impact of the measure was on the rights of the church, especially the monasteries, and it solved the immediate problem of what would become of the jurisdictional powers of a dissolved abbey. The act was also less comprehensive than its preamble suggests. It effectively preserved the authority of the palatine bishopric of Durham and the archbishop of York's control of Hexhamshire. Even more important, it preserved the palatine identity of the county of Lancaster. The only palatinate to go was Chester—redundant now that Wales was to be shired.

It must also be noted that where uniformity was promoted, it was not necessarily in the nation's interest. As has been seen, Henry depended heavily on a peerage which through much of the country had become a service-nobility. Instances where particular aristocrats fell foul of the king were in no way part of any deliberate anti-aristocratic policy. Yet on the border an older breed of noble was needed, possessed of and willing to use *manred* to maintain order and fend off the Scots. Henry failed to see this different requirement and treated some of the leading northern families with grave suspicion precisely because they were not on the service-noblemen model. Thomas, third Baron Dacre, who was warden of the west marches for forty years, was made warden-general by Henry VIII and built his 'power' into an effective bulwark against the Scots, but was nevertheless sacked and heavily fined in 1525 because he had not imposed order of the quality expected in a southern county. His son and successor William was tried for treason in 1534 on account of the cross-border ties he had built up, to the benefit of both England and Scotland. In 1537 the sixth earl of Northumberland gave up and abandoned the Percy estates to the crown.

Thanks to doubts about northern nobles and an unwillingness to fund them properly, Henry was forced to turn to 'mean men' such as Sir Thomas Wharton, but they did not possess the requisite local clout and had frequently to be supported by royal lieutenants from the south. As Edward Seymour, earl of Hertford, pointed out when trying to evade a commission as warden-general, 'he that shall serve here had neide to be both kyn and alied emong them of thies parties and suche oon as hathe and dothe bere rule in the countreye by reason of his landes or otherwise' (Bain, 1.lxii–lxiii). The result of the king's refusal to collaborate with suitable local magnates was that, when he died, border defence was more expensive and less effective and English officials began to write of 'the decay of the borders'. Wharton had to be replaced by Lord Dacre in 1549.

One development which did less for law and order in the border than might appear was the emergence of the council of the north. As with Wales there were earlier precedents for this, but its continuous history began only in 1525 with the organization by Wolsey of a standing council to support the duke of Richmond's appointment as the king's lieutenant in the north, and with authority over the marches as well as Yorkshire. In 1530 Richmond and his estates were hived off and Cuthbert Tunstal, bishop of Durham, became president with authority only over Yorkshire. When this council was tested by the Pilgrimage of Grace it failed entirely (many of its members were involved with the pilgrims), so in 1537 a further reform produced a properly organized bureaucratic body. Its initial remit extended beyond Yorkshire but its responsibilities for the border fluctuated and the system of wardens of the marches remained unchanged.

The Irish problem

Whether or not Henry consciously pursued ideas of the unitary state, Cromwell's legislation did integrate the border regions and the rest of England. In the lordship of Ireland the situation was far more complex, as a report to the king explained in about 1515. 'Folke dayly subgett to the Kinges lawes' occupied Dublin and its hinterland known as the Pale, between 20 and 40 miles deep. The 'Kinges Iryshe enymyes' held Ulster and Connaught plus important enclaves in the mountainous areas south of Dublin and in the far west. Here society was Gaelic-speaking, pastoral, clan-based, and according to the report 'lyveyth onely by the swerde'. The rest of Ireland was occupied by the king's 'Englyshe rebelles', holders of marcher franchises carved out by medieval English colonists where obedience to the king's overlordship was decidedly flexible. The report envisaged the disciplining of the 'wylde Iryshe' through a wholesale militarization of the loyalist population plus renewed immigration. Military expeditions on their own were useless. 'An armye that is moveing temperall for a season and not perpetuall, shalle never profyt the King in Ireland withoute the Kinges subgettes of the land be put in ordre, for assone as the army is agoo, the Kinges obeysaunce is' (*State Papers, Henry VIII*, 3.1–31). It was an opinion which Henry's father had shared: 'little advantage or profit hath grown of such armies and captains as have been sent for the reduction of Ireland' (Bayne and Dunham, 46–7).

For the first decade of his reign Henry followed his father in leaving the greatest of the marchers, the Fitzgerald earls of Kildare, to provide the deputy and enhance the king's power by enhancing their own. Then, possibly inspired by the report of *c*.1515, Henry began to take a personal and novel interest in Irish affairs. He summoned Gerald Fitzgerald, the ninth earl, to the royal court in 1519, detained him, and in 1520 sent over the earl of Surrey as lord lieutenant. What was novel about this was that Henry entertained the possibility of drawing Gaelic Ireland into the Tudor state by 'sober waies, politique driftes and amiable persuasions founded in lawe and reason', although characteristically he also envisaged the crown recovering its long defunct feudal rights (*State Papers, Henry VIII*, 3.52). However, the earl of Surrey advocated the traditional policy of compulsion and Henry rapidly lost interest in the call for men and money, particularly as his attention shifted to war with France. He recalled the earl to England saying:

We and our Counsaill, taking regard aswell to the merval-ouse great charges that we yerely susteyne, by enterteigne-ment of you, our Lieutenaunte, with the retynue under you there, as also the litle effecte that succedeth therof have clerely perceyved and in maner determyned that to employe...any other English Lieutenaunte with lyke retynue as ye have nowe, shulde be frustratorie and con-sumpcion of treasour in vayne. (ibid., 3.90–91)

He had come up against the rock which would obstruct all Tudor ambition for Ireland.

This recognition of realities marks the point at which the king's first personal initiative came to a halt. The letter was drafted by Wolsey, but the minister's short-term alternatives turned out no more successfully. Two years of Piers Butler, earl of Ormond, as deputy was followed by four years of his rival, Kildare, and despite a commission sent to compromise their quarrel, the Kildare–Ormond rivalry continued (backed by partisans at the English court). In 1528 came the settlement between Piers Butler and Anne Boleyn's father of their com-peting claims to the Butler peerage (with Butler becoming earl of Ossory) and Henry, believing that Kildare was trying to force himself back into office, overrode Wolsey and sent Ossory back as deputy. The situation deteriorated further and in June 1529 the duke of Richmond was made lieutenant with a council in support—the expedient which in 1525 had been tried in the north of England with the duke and in Wales with his half-sister.

Sir William Skeffington went with a small body of troops to represent Richmond, but within the year the king cut his funds—money again. The element of court faction became even more important and in 1532 led to the return of Kildare as deputy. Thomas Cromwell also entered the picture, but the new minister came with no preconceived policy except suspicion of Kildare, and he built up the Butlers and the Pale administrators against the earl. In February 1534 Kildare eventually complied with yet another order to come to London and Skeffington took his place in July, but with no new policies and predictably weak forces. A new complication also emerged, the need to have Ireland repudiate papal authority. Then, in a massive miscalculation of Geraldine indispensability, Kildare's son, 'Silken Thomas', publicly denounced royal policies and besieged Dublin Castle. Kildare himself was sent to the Tower where he died, and Silken Thomas, now earl of Kildare, presented the rising as a crusade against heresy, even though no religious change had occurred. There was widespread support from the clergy and many palesmen and the king's own officials joined in too. Charles V did not respond to pleas to intervene, but by the autumn only Dublin, Kilkenny, and Waterford stood out for Henry. However, Skeffington arrived in October with 2300 men and brought the Pale gentry back into line; and when Kildare's main stronghold surrendered in March 1535, he massacred the garrison ('the pardon of Maynooth'). Kildare surrendered in August on promise of his life and was sent to London. He and his five uncles were executed in February 1537 in the aftermath of the Pilgrimage of Grace, and the destruction of the Kildare ascendancy forced Henry to find another way to rule the lordship, and Gaelic lords to reorder their alliances likewise.

Henry abandoned once and for all the attempt to achieve satisfactory government by aristocratic delegation; henceforward the deputy would have to be English and backed by a standing army and a council under English control. Skeffington died in December 1535 and was followed by Lord Leonard Grey who called the Irish 'Reformation' parliament in May. The first session passed the appropriate reformation statutes but royal money bills were rejected in September and the king had to do a deal with the gentry over monastic dissolution. The Irish council called for conquest but Henry decided that policy should be limited to what the revenue from Ireland would pay for. Reforming commissioners who kept close contact with Cromwell were sent in September 1537. They cut down the army (and hence limited operations in the marches) and instead fortified the Pale as an English enclave. There was to be no more interference in Gaelic Ireland; within the Englishry, Cromwellian administrative reform was to lay a firm base for the future. Financial inquiries showed a rise in the nominal revenue, thanks to the religious dissolutions which were possible in areas of English influence, but the actual income declined and the administration fell into debt. Not that financial stringency was all bad. It did put a stop to the more extravagant notions about integration.

This policy of treating the Pale as a fortified bastion like the Pale of Calais proved unsustainable because it was impossible to ignore the vacuum of authority in the marches and Gaelic Ireland which the fall of the Geraldines had produced. There, something like a Hobbesian state of nature prevailed with no Leviathan to discipline individual magnates and clan overlords.

Lord Grey therefore reverted to the Kildare policy of putting pressure on and doing deals with the Gaelic chiefs, only to be recalled to England, tried, and executed. Cromwell, too, had now fallen and the next deputy, Sir Anthony St Leger, therefore had considerably more freedom. He was an administrator, not a soldier, and a major success. He pursued a policy of inducing the Gaelic chiefs to accept Henry as sovereign in return for a recognition of their title to land and significant reductions in the king's theoretical feudal claims. In June 1541 the Irish parliament facilitated this by recognizing Henry as 'king' of Ireland, a change (greeted by public celebrations in Dublin) which incidentally also extinguished papal claims to Ireland. Henceforward the 'Kinges Iryshe enymyes' would be his subjects and English policy would be an 'all-Ireland' policy. The affinity to the settlement in Wales is clear but Henry was anything but pleased. 'Considre whither it be either honor or wisdom for Us to take upon Us that title of a King, and not to have revenues there, suffycyent to maynteyn the state of the same' (*State Papers, Henry VIII*, 3.331). Revenue had to be found and since deals with the Gaelic chiefs involved the surrender of what he still believed were valuable royal rights, they must be stopped immediately. In future, a contribution to the revenue must be agreed in advance.

Despite royal annoyance the policy which became known as 'surrender and regrant' did produce results. The Gaelic chieftains came to court, made a submission to Henry, and were invested with their lands, and with titles. The deputy was able to arbitrate in a number of long-running Gaelic feuds and practical benefit came to the English crown in 1544 when Henry was able to enlist Irish troops, the first recourse for centuries to what would be a major recruiting ground for the English crown.

Admittedly there were problems. Change came too slowly, some of the English administrators hankered after expropriation (a pressure which would grow), and Gaelic power structures were hard to disentangle. And there was always the problem of money. The kingdom's debt reached £12,000 sterling and yearly subsidies were still needed—in part to make up for official peculation.

Henry VIII's reign nevertheless ended with Ireland relatively settled. It had also been fundamentally changed. The old policy of maintaining an English bridgehead into a culturally divided Ireland had been replaced by a commitment to the reduction and Anglicization of the whole island. To a degree that reflected the king's thinking when he sent Surrey in 1520, but it would be too much to say that he had arrived at this by planning and intention. Nor were matters stable. The commitment to Anglicization was open-ended and would require further progress in the imposition of religious reform which had yet to touch Gaelic Ireland. What is more, the obstacle he faced in 1520 was still there. The effective government of Ireland involved a continuous drain on the English exchequer.

The fall of Thomas Cromwell

While king and minister were busy with legislation and initiatives which, for good or ill, had long-term effects for the British Isles, Henry's private life continued to create problems. Despite any grief he may have had at the death of Jane Seymour on 24 October 1537, the search for a fourth royal consort began within days. At least nine European partners were considered—and the consequent diplomatic implications of each—before, as has been seen, Henry's choice eventually lighted on Anne, the sister of the duke of Cleves, a decision determined by a dangerous *rapprochement* between the emperor and the king of France.

The marriage took place on 6 January 1540 and it lasted six months and a day. Henry took an instant dislike to the 24-year-old Anne. Despite tradition, this can scarcely have been because of her looks. Portraits suggest that she was hardly less pleasing than Henry's other wives and the 'Flanders mare' sneer is an eighteenth-century invention. The more probable explanation is again Henry's egoism. At their first meeting Anne thoroughly punctured his self-esteem. He had swept into her room at Rochester, disguised and bearing gifts, a 48-year-old trying to recapture chivalric youth, but instead of an elegant sophisticate who would recognize this courtly trope, Henry found himself embracing a dowdy provincial, with neither personality, wit, nor knowledge of English, who then turned away to continue watching a bull being baited in the courtyard below. And he had only himself to blame, having been warned that in conformity with German court culture, Anne neither sang nor played and had been brought up to eschew 'good cheer' (*LP Henry VIII*, 14/2, no. 33). A deflated Henry tried to cancel the marriage plans but diplomatic inevitability prevailed. However, as Wolsey had said, an idea once planted in Henry's head was almost impossible to eradicate and nothing that Anne was or did changed the king's mind. Not that she did much, since she was innocent of the arts of seduction and despite sleeping with the king for several months remained a virgin. They were divorced in July 1540 on grounds of non-consummation and the evidence Henry gave to his doctors suggests that during this marriage he was impotent. Anne Boleyn had reported similar inadequacy from time to time.

On 28 July, three weeks after the annulment of the Cleves marriage, Thomas Cromwell was beheaded and the common supposition has been that the two events were the joint consequence of Cromwell's misjudgement in making the Cleves marriage. In fact the initiative had been as much Henry's, if not more. The failure of the Cleves marriage was, nevertheless, ominous for the minister. Henry's eye fell on Katherine Howard, the frisky niece of the duke of Norfolk, so allowing the duke and the rest of the faction opposed to the minister to dangle Katherine before the king, much as Jane Seymour had been offered for sale. The prospect of a Howard in the royal bed was abhorrent to Cromwell and although Henry had told him in late March that there was an 'obstacle' to consummating the marriage, Cromwell chose to encourage Anne to be more vivacious, rather than taking prompt action to free Henry from a union which made increasingly less diplomatic sense as Charles V and François I drifted apart. Perhaps Cromwell relied too much on the favour implicit in Henry's final promotions, elevation in April 1540 to the earldom of Essex and appointment as lord great chamberlain. If so, he was wrong. Howard and his allies increasingly had the royal ear and poisoned it with the story that Cromwell's reforms cloaked Anabaptist opinions—a charge bolstered by reports of the number of 'sacramentarians' (those who denied transubstantiation) who had infiltrated the ranks of the reformers at Calais. Cromwell counter-attacked with allegations of crypto-popery but he was arrested, condemned by act of attainder, and executed.

The royal legacy

Political changes and royal marriages, 1540–1547

The fall of Cromwell in June 1540 put an end to the second period of kingly rule via a chief minister and ushered in a further, and this time enduring, period of government via a council. It was, however, not the council which Cromwell had sidelined before the break with Rome. The risings of 1536 had strongly criticized the minister and other counsellors 'of low byrth and small reputation' (*LP Henry VIII*, 11, no. 705(1)). What is more, the risings had been too much to be handled by king and minister alone. Leading magnates had therefore been called in to join a war cabinet to issue instructions and pronouncements during the risings, making as little mention as possible of the hated Cromwell, Cranmer, and Cromwell's ally Sir Thomas Audley. The body proved its worth and quickly became a permanent 'privy council' of notables and office holders. On the other hand, Cromwell was not immediately ousted. Henry was not ready to give up the use of a principal minister, nor was Cromwell ready to share power with other counsellors, particularly because many of them were bitterly hostile to the religious changes Henry was promoting under his and Cranmer's influence. The consequence was a period of some three and a half years when Cromwell was dominant, but always having to guard his back, and when the privy council was denied bureaucratic machinery of its own, that would have allowed it to operate as an executive.

Nevertheless, the existence of a majority on the council hostile to Cromwell had had its effect on Henry, as the traditionalists exploited the access which his interest in Katherine Howard gave them. Cromwell's arrest actually took place at a council meeting. Some months later Charles de Marillac reported Henry as saying that his counsellors 'upon light pretext, by false accusations, had made him put to death the most faithful servants he ever had' (*LP Henry VIII*, 16, no. 590). Nevertheless, Henry continued with the privy council format, although in the final months of the reign there are signs that Sir William Paget was on the way to becoming his third chief minister.

Henry's marriage to Katherine Howard, his fifth, took place on 28 July 1540, the day of Cromwell's execution, and the king was rejuvenated, 'so amorous of her that he knows not how to make sufficient demonstrations of his affection, and caresses her more than he did the others'. Katherine played up to her sugar daddy. Gossip told how 'the king had no wife who made him spend so much money in dresses and jewels as she did, and every day some fresh caprice' (Hume, 77). He allowed an influx of Howard relatives on to her staff and conservatives dominated the court. In the following June, Henry set off with Katherine on a huge progress via Lincoln to the city of York, exhibiting all his royal magnificence to seal the pacification of the north. There was a set-back when James V, who had been invited to meet his uncle at York, did not turn up, but the king continued on his triumphant way, finding time *en route* to plan new fortifications for Hull. On his return he ordered public thanks-giving for his marriage to be made on All Saints' day, only to receive a letter in his pew next day telling him that when he married her, the queen had not been a virgin. Henry broke down and Katherine was placed under house arrest. Interro-gation revealed not only pre-nuptial misconduct but improper behaviour after her marriage and at least the intent to commit adultery with a royal favourite, Thomas Culpeper. In December the men involved were executed and Katherine and her confi-dante Lady Rochford, the widow of George Boleyn, followed on 13 February 1542. The Howards who had known about her early misconduct were sent to the Tower. Norfolk retired to his house in Suffolk and wrote bewailing 'the most abhomynable dedes done by 2 of my niesys agaynst Your Highnes' (*State Papers, Henry VIII*, 2.721).

Henry remained a widower until 12 July 1543 when he mar-ried the childless, twice-widowed Katherine Parr. Although Katherine was pleasing and graceful, this time Henry was choosing on grounds of companionship, not looks. Katherine was well-educated for a woman of her time and rank, of reformist opinions but judiciously expressed, a good conversa-tionalist who knew how to handle the king and knew her duty, even though she had been hoping to marry the younger and more exciting Thomas Seymour, Prince Edward's uncle. Her motto, 'To be useful in all I do', says it all. If Henry's final years had some element of tranquillity, he owed it to Katherine.

Return to war

In the 1530s domestic priorities governed royal policy. After the Katherine Howard débâcle—perhaps partly in compensation—external concerns came once more to occupy the king's mind.

The Scottish border certainly called for action. Theoretically England was at peace with Scotland—a treaty had been signed in 1534 following an outburst of raids and counter-raids on the borders in late 1532 and 1533. However, disorder was endemic and in July 1542 Henry decided to give the Scottish border reivers 'oon shrewd turn for an other' (*State Papers, Henry VIII*, 4.206). When the resulting punitive raid was defeated at Haddon Rig, Henry ordered a bigger incursion in November. Tit for tat ended dramatically on 23 November when the Scottish riposte was heavily defeated at Solway Moss and a number of significant prisoners captured, and even more decisively when James V died suddenly on 14 December, leaving the Scottish crown to his week-old daughter, Mary. Europe, however, was also beginning to present diplomatic and military opportunities. Open hostilities between Charles V and François I had resumed in June 1542 and this gave Henry possibilities to manoeuvre and strut on the international stage which he had not enjoyed since the 1520s. In February 1543, despite the potential of the Scottish situation, Henry agreed with Charles V on joint invasions of France, and he dispatched 5000 men in June.

In the following month the war with Scotland was ended by the treaties of Greenwich, but Henry had not got all he wanted and five months later he resumed hostilities. In the following spring a combined operation involving 14,000 troops wreaked havoc on the Scottish lowlands. But a month later Henry invaded France with almost 40,000 men and he joined them in person in mid-July. Montreuil and Boulogne were invested and the latter surrendered on 14 September, four days before Charles and François concluded the bilateral peace of Crépy. Through 1545 England fought on alone, defeating invasion attempts and attacks on Boulogne, and answering the arrival of French reinforcements in Scotland with a massive counter-raid. Eventually stalemate and lack of funds forced the belligerents to make peace at Camp (otherwise Ardres) in June 1546.

The sense to be made of all this has been the subject of considerable debate. One theory is that Henry's policies towards France and Scotland were distinct in origin and affected each other only because the two countries were old allies. An explanation more frequently heard is that the king's principal objective was the unification of Britain. With legislation in 1536 ending the distinctiveness of Wales and the 1541 declaration that Henry was king of Ireland, attempting to annex Scotland can appear to be the last piece in the jigsaw. On this hypothesis, France was attacked in an attempt to neutralize 'the auld alliance'. However, judged by the respective levels of military commitment, France not Scotland appears to have been the major target, and as has been seen neither the shiring of Wales nor the upgrading of the Irish title was inspired by constitutional aspirations.

An alternative interpretation of foreign policy sees Henry's cross-channel assault in 1544 as a return to his earlier desire to reopen the Hundred Years' War and achieve military glory at the expense of France, with the raids across the border merely attempts to pre-empt Scottish intervention in support of an ally. That military glory certainly was a motive in Henry's policy to France is evident. It was inevitable that 'a hero king' would make attempts to recover land which the English crown had held as recently as his grandfather's youth. Along with honour went profit. The significant pension which France had paid the English king since 1475 had not been honoured for several years and by 1542 the arrears were more than £200,000. Overall, however, the best explanation of Henry's motivation is dynasticism. Early modern rulers saw it as a moral duty to acquire and retain what belonged to them by legal right, with the related obligation to advance the future interests and standing of their families.

Such concerns motivated Charles and François. So too Henry. When it suited him, or when he was in no position to take action, he could make light of his claim to the crown of France, but this was not so at other times. Towards Scotland in the 1540s dynastic considerations were paramount. James was the next legitimate heir to the English crown after Prince Edward. As James committed Scotland more and more to links with France and to Catholic orthodoxy, the potential threat he presented to a dubious English succession was obvious. His replacement by Mary, queen of Scots, raised issues that were different but still dynastic. Was this not a golden opportunity to add Scotland to the English crown through marriage, the technique which had brought about Charles V's world empire? Did not the contrary to this—the danger that another European power would use marriage with Mary to annex Scotland—provide an even greater reason to intervene? Alternatively, should Scottish weakness be exploited to reassert England's claim to suzerainty north of the border or 'at the leaste the domynion on thisside the Frethe [Forth]?' (*State Papers, Henry VIII*, 4.319).

Honour and dynastic tradition drew Henry to attack France; dynastic opportunity and dynastic danger drew him to give Scotland priority. In typical fashion he attempted to have the best of all worlds. Some of the Scottish nobles captured at Solway Moss were persuaded to support him ('the assured lords') and with their help Henry secured the apparent triumph of a provision in the treaties of Greenwich that Edward and Mary should marry. However, his immediate intention was clearly to dominate Scotland. The negotiations might talk about a union and a single kingdom called 'Britain', but that was shorthand for Tudor family expansion. The Scots stalled and Henry, angry at the delay, had recourse to the big stick. Given Scottish weakness, that might have succeeded if he had deployed the biggest stick he had, but the king reserved that for France. As a result he fell between two stools. The attempt to compel Scotland to allow the marriage was reduced to spasmodic punitive expeditions and the attack on France yielded Boulogne. In 1545 not only did France reply with an attack on the south coast—which cost Henry his flagship, the *Mary Rose*—but it also put troops into Scotland! The peace made in 1546 gave the king nothing north of the border, and although he was to retain Boulogne for eight years, the town was, as his advisers had told him, the whitest of white elephants. Henry, attempting a grand slam, had ended with one minor trick.

Shaping the future

Modern historians have often written as though, in contrast to the dramatic changes of the thirteen years which preceded them, the last seven years of Henry's reign have had little importance. This is a mistake. From 1540 onwards not only were the earlier changes 'road tested', but the legacy of these last years substantially determined the agenda of the next twenty. And an evil legacy it was. After the break with Rome the king had become an active supreme head who developed his own very self-confident, eclectic, and at times highly idiosyncratic theology. This, however, was no recipe for continuity once he was gone. His young son was left in mid-stream between positions which can now, without anachronism, be characterized as Catholic and protestant, and, moreover, Henry (as we shall see) had had him tutored by reformers and would bequeath him a privy council dominated by them. Mary fared no better when she became queen and wished to turn the clock back. She quickly swept away the recent changes associated with her brother's regime but then found herself frustrated by the much more fundamental destruction and anti-traditionalism of her father's reign.

Equally destabilizing was the plan Henry laid in 1536 to circumvent the prohibition on illegitimate children inheriting property, in particular the crown. This barred the duke of Richmond and so too his two half-sisters because their father was adamantly convinced that neither of the mothers had been married to him, an objection which the second Succession Act spelled out in uncompromising fashion. That, however, threatened the end of the Tudor line with Henry being succeeded by James V of Scotland (Edward had yet to be born). Clauses were therefore added to that same Succession Act recognizing that in the absence of legitimate children of his own, the king had the right to name a successor. This hitherto unheard-of prerogative meant that although Richmond, Mary, and Elizabeth were barred from succeeding by inheritance, they could nevertheless succeed by being nominated. Whatever plans he had for Richmond were cut short by the boy's death within days of the statute becoming law, but then Henry began to hint that he might use the act to nominate Mary. He eventually made his intentions public in 1544 when a third Succession Act specifically named Mary and Elizabeth to succeed after Edward. By thus substituting bastards for his legitimate collateral heirs, the Stuarts of Scotland and the Grey family in England, Henry was driving a coach and horses through the common law of inheritance and putting the monarchy itself at risk. The pilgrims immediately protested that 'never was there known in this realm no such law' (quoted in Bateson, 563). The affront to common law provided the rationale for the attempt to put Jane Grey on the throne in 1553 rather than Mary. It was also at the core of the succession problem which bedevilled Elizabeth's reign. Only the accession of James Stuart in 1603 put an end to the evil consequences of Henry VIII's hubris.

The foreign adventuring of Henry VIII's last years was an equally poisonous bequest. Nor was this simply his folly in allowing the potential dynastic danger from Scotland to become entangled with French resentment at the insult which was Boulogne. The war had been massively expensive—£1,600,000 plus the costs of garrisons and fortifications. For thirty years population growth had been producing inflation but government expenditure on this scale gave a huge boost to the price rise. By 1544 inflation had risen nineteen points. In order to fund the war the king first imposed the highest level of parliamentary and non-parliamentary taxation since the fourteenth century. That provided a quarter of the cost. Perhaps as much again was made from the sale of former church lands, with important long-term social consequences. The remainder, except for limited borrowing in London and abroad, was obtained through coinage manipulation—the so-called 'great debasement' which began in 1544 and saw coins being made smaller and their fineness reduced by 16 per cent for gold and 64 per cent for silver. Fortunately much of the debased money which Henry struck—in effect 'printed'—was spent abroad, but English economic stability was affected and by the time he died the index had risen a further twenty-three points, to nearly twice its level of 1509. Debasement also damaged overseas trade. Between January 1544 and January value.

Henry's evil legacy also extended to politics and government. The privy council had replaced Thomas Cromwell, but it was deeply divided. At one level the division was over religion, to influence the king towards maintaining tradition or towards protecting and advancing reform. However, at another level the issue was positioning for the next reign and a royal minority which could not long be delayed. From time to time the factions attempted coups of the sort which had been successful in the past. Thomas Cranmer was the target of determined scheming throughout 1543 in which Bishop Gardiner, Sir John Baker, another conservative privy councillor, and the duke of Norfolk sought to exploit complaints by traditionalists at Windsor and in Kent. The climax came, probably in November, when Henry did give way to pressure and sanction action against the archbishop. Within hours he had changed his mind, fetched Cranmer out of bed, and given him a ring to produce—the token Henry customarily used to signal that he was taking personal charge of a case. He also read Cranmer a lesson on what would have happened otherwise:

> Doo you not thincke that yf thei have you ones in prison, iii or iiij false knaves wilbe procured to witnes againste you and to condemne you, whiche els now being at your libertie dare not ones open thair lipps or appere before your face. Noo, not so, my lorde, I have better regarde unto you than to permitte your enemyes so to overthrowe you. (Nichols, 255)

A few weeks later there was a counter-attack which took the life of Germain Gardiner—the bishop of Winchester's nephew and secretary and his agent against Cranmer—but the bishop himself was warned and saved himself by getting to the king before he could be arrested.

As the 1540s proceeded, new figures emerged to lead the political élite, notably Prince Edward's uncle Edward Seymour, earl of Hertford, and John Dudley, Viscount Lisle. They were cautious reformers but their influence on the privy council was limited because from 1542 they were busy on military matters, Hertford as the king's principal general and Lisle at the admiralty, both high in favour. As peace in 1546 became certain, the prospect of their return tilting the balance of influence, forced the traditionalists to make another attempt to discredit reform in Henry's eyes. In April a popular preacher, Dr Edward Crome, denied the existence of purgatory and the ensuing inquiry dragged in others, including Hugh Latimer. Burnings were followed by the arrest of an outspoken reformist gentlewoman, Anne Askew, who was known to have links with the like-minded ladies around Queen Katherine, including Hertford's wife and the wife of Sir Antony Denny, the reformist chief gentleman of the privy chamber, but despite being racked by hands of Thomas Wriothesley, the lord chancellor, Anne implicated nobody. Then the queen herself became a target. Finding the king in a thoroughly bad mood because of his diseased leg and being bested in theological argument by Katherine Parr, Gardiner persuaded the annoyed husband that she too should be investigated for heresy. Timely warning allowed the queen to make her peace with Henry before the guard arrived to arrest her. With the return of his commanders the traditionalists steadily lost ground as the king spent much time in their company. Either by maladroitness or misrepresentation Gardiner fell from favour, Wriothesley changed sides, and Norfolk's injudicious son, Henry Howard, earl of Surrey, said enough to be arrested in December for treason, followed by his father.

The earl was executed on 21 January but his father survived because the bill attainting him received the royal assent only a few hours before the king's own death.

The king's will

It was in the context of this final factional battle that Henry revised his last will and testament on 30 December 1546. It was authenticated by the dry stamp, a form of signature by proxy which Henry had introduced in 1545 to save himself trouble. This system was in theory open to abuse, but the will is undoubtedly genuine. Arguments that it was stamped only after the king became incapacitated, or even after he was dead, do not stand up to analysis. The king confirmed Edward as heir and after Edward, Mary and Elizabeth, though the girls were to lose their places in the succession if they married without the written permission of a majority of privy councillors. Next in line he put the Grey and Clifford families, descendants of Mary, his younger sister. The granddaughter of Henry's elder sister, Margaret—Mary, queen of Scots—was not mentioned, though presumably she qualified in the final remainder to the next rightful heirs. To govern the country during his son's minority, Henry nominated sixteen executors who were to function as Edward's privy council, and since sixteen might be too few for day-to-day business, he named a further twelve to be counsellors to the sixteen as and when required.

Henry's will provoked discussion in the reigns of Mary and Elizabeth and also in modern times. Some historians have argued that because traditionalist and anti-traditionalist councillors were roughly equal in numbers, Henry's intention was to rule from the grave and preserve his individual religious policy. This, however, ignores the fact that political weight and leadership were all on the side of the reformers. Others have made the improbable suggestion that Henry did not know of, or was not concerned with, religious affinities. Nor is it convincing that the will simply froze the political *status quo* of late December 1546, or that it was imposed by the reformist faction on a fast-failing king. All the evidence suggests that, though seriously unwell, Henry was in control. In December he annotated the charges against Surrey with his own hand and as late as 17 January he was fully in command when receiving the French and imperial ambassadors. All in all, the conclusion has to be that, in deciding on his son's counsellors, his intention was to limit the influence of religious conservatism. And the reason is not hard to seek. Recovering the supreme headship of the church in England had been his greatest achievement, and conservatives could not be trusted to preserve that in its full force. It was a conviction of which Henry had given sign several years earlier when he decided to appoint the moderate reformers Richard Cox and John Cheke as Edward's tutors when, as the boy put it later, he ceased to be brought up 'amoung the wemen' (Nichols, *Literary Remains*, 2.209).

Henry did not name a protector. The office had unhappy overtones. However, councils of regency also had a poor history and were easily vitiated by faction. To guard against this Henry was careful to provide that the named membership of the privy council could not be changed and that decisions had to be taken by simple majority vote of 'such of them as shall then be alive' (Rymer, *Foedera*, 15.115). In other words his designated counsellors were locked into a need to collaborate. Given that, the king made it quite clear that this restricted body had full plenary power to act as it thought best. Henry clearly expected the earl of Hertford to lead—he gave the stamped will to him for safe keeping and he created him earl marshal and treasurer. However, fettered by the majority rule and with no opportunity to pack the council with their own nominees, neither Hertford nor any other regent would, Henry hoped, be able to abuse royal authority.

Henry died at Whitehall Palace in the early hours of Friday 28 January 1547. His body was embalmed and lay in state in the presence chamber at Whitehall. On 14 February it was moved by stages to Windsor where it was buried in the morning of the 16th in the vault of St George's Chapel, next to the grave of Jane Seymour.

The royal magnificence: images and reality

Wealth and culture

In 1546 Henry did not go bankrupt as Charles V and François I did on more than one occasion, but he died in debt. However, against this had to be set his enormous accumulated wealth. The remarkable inventory made after his death lists nearly 20,000 items. The tone is set by the first, his gold crown weighing nearly 7 lb and adorned with some 340 precious stones. His gold and silver candlesticks alone weighed a quarter of a ton; he had hundreds of tapestries; thousands of yards of cloth of gold were in store, ready to make into his elaborately ornamented costumes. Beside this fortune in chattels must be set his houses: he inherited thirteen; when he died he owned over fifty, most of which he acquired after 1530.

Not only did he acquire property, but from the time of Wolsey's fall Henry developed a passion for construction and reconstruction. In consequence, for much of his reign he lived in a series of building sites. His underlying determination was to display his status as one of Europe's 'big three'. That, in particular, required continual development at his three greatest palaces: Greenwich, perhaps his favourite, built by his father; Hampton Court, which Wolsey gave him and on which Henry spent £62,000 in ten years; and Whitehall, which he extended over 23 acres from a nucleus of the London house of the archdiocese of York which Wolsey had rebuilt. And as soon as Henry had designed, he wanted the finished result, with the consequence that what he constructed was often impressively disguised jerry-building. Not that better quality work would necessarily have been wiser; Henry regularly wanted to change what had been built, immediately he saw it.

Henry's most remarkable venture followed his decision in 1537 to create Hampton Court Chase, an enormous hunting-ground upstream of the palace on the opposite bank of the Thames. A preserve of this size required a subsidiary hunting-lodge, so Henry swept away the village, church, and manor house of Cuddington near Esher and built Nonsuch, as its name indicates, the palace to eclipse all others, in particular the famous châteaux of François I. What justified its name was the exterior of plaster-stucco panels bearing classical scenes and motifs in high relief, between borders of carved and gilded slate. Most of the craftsmen on Henry's buildings were Flemish but the Nonsuch exterior was worked on by Nicholas Bellin of Modena whom he had purloined from working for François I on Fontainebleau. A design by Bellin, possibly for the interior of Nonsuch, is clearly related to the Galerie François Ier at Fontainebleau, so the Italian artistic influence on the palace via France may have been considerable.

Henry's own tastes in fine art are hard to pin down. He was possibly something of a squirrel, collecting what took his fancy. Whitehall was decorated with history paintings of his triumphs, and Henry owned hundreds of pictures, principally portraits and religious paintings on largely predictable themes. However, he was undoubtedly attracted by the new Renaissance fashions of which Thomas Wolsey had been the great ambassador. The royal plate was often decorated in the antique style and so too the jewellery designed for him, although nothing is known of the designs the king himself produced. He employed intaglio cutters and possessed the earliest portrait medals known in England, although here Italian influence was mediated via Germany. Renaissance motifs were used in decorating the walls and windows of his palaces although they were balanced by a riot of traditional heraldic badges and symbols.

Henry engaged a number of foreign artists. The most successful Italian in his service was Antonio Toto who became sergeant-painter, though Henry employed half-a-dozen others including Pietro Torrigiani who designed a tomb and highly Italianate altarpiece at Westminster commemorating the king's father. The tomb commissioned by Wolsey from Benedetto da Rovezzano was appropriated by Henry and substantially (but not completely) finished by Giovanni da Maiano. For miniatures, the king used the Horenbout family from Flanders, but it was Anne Boleyn who introduced Hans Holbein the younger into the royal circle. After the latter's death in 1543 Henry recruited Guillim Scrotes who had worked for Mary of Hungary, the regent of the Habsburg Netherlands. Much of the time of the royal artists was devoted to ephemeral court entertainments, while Holbein appears never to have been fully appreciated and to have been regarded as the equivalent of a superior photographer.

Holbein nevertheless created the definitive image of Henry in heroic classical pose. The original semi-profile face mask survives as the head and shoulders portrait of 1537 in the Thyssen collection and in the full-length cartoon of the figure of Henry for the privy chamber wall painting of the following year, showing Henry with his father and mother and Jane Seymour. The realized fresco was destroyed by fire in 1698 but surviving small-scale copies show that Holbein switched to a direct frontal image for the finished work. Numerous later versions of this image survive, head and shoulders, three-quarter length, and full length. Holbein used it himself for the cartoon of Henry and the barber–surgeons and for his part in the associated (but composite) painting. Appearances of Henry in groups by anonymous artists include *The Family of Henry VIII* (Royal Collection) and *Charles V and Henry VIII* (private collection), while Lambert Barnard's panel paintings in Chichester Cathedral include a scene of Henry restoring the privileges of the see to Bishop Robert Sherborn. Henry also appears in a number of history paintings, such as the *Field of Cloth of Gold* (Royal Collection). There are two earlier anonymous half-length portraits (*c.*1520 and *c.*1527) and one of about 1535 by Joos van Cleeve (Royal Collection). There are in addition two post-Holbein patterns, one full-length, possibly by Lucas Horenbout. Horenbout also produced a miniature dated 1526–7. A miniature by Holbein shows Henry as Solomon and so too a window in the chapel of King's College, Cambridge. He appears in a number of illuminated manuscripts: the great tournament roll of Westminster, the procession of the peers in the 1512 parliament, the king's own psalter (playing the part of King David), the Wriothesley Garter book and the black book of the Garter, and on various legal and diplomatic documents. A drawing survives of Henry as an infant and another showing the adult Henry in the privy chamber; an engraving by Cornelis Matsys depicts Henry in the last years of his life. In print, Henry appears on the frontispiece in both the Coverdale Bible and the Great Bible. And there is also the conjectural terracotta bust by Guido Mazzoni. Two portrait medals of Henry exist and where the king's head appears on coins, it was clearly intended as a portrait. The sculptured relief of Henry at the Field of Cloth of Gold on the Hotel du Bourgthéroulde in Rouen was damaged in 1944.

Thomas More and the humanist scholar Erasmus enthused that the younger Henry was a patron of good letters. He certainly employed humanists at court and in government, both foreigners and Englishmen such as More and Richard Pace. Henry was also a target for aspiring authors: many of the contemporary works he owned were presentation copies. Although there is evidence that he often preferred being read to rather than to read himself, and that Anne Boleyn marked selected passages for him, the king liked to picture himself as a *littérateur*. He had long and enjoyable conversations with visiting scholars and many of his books carry annotations by him. He was also the first English king since Alfred to write and publish a book—even though with help—and, as has been seen, he did work on many of his government's pronouncements on religion. Henry had a library at Hampton Court and at least two at Greenwich, while the main collection was at Whitehall. In all he possessed some 1500 titles in both manuscript and print. Some he had inherited, others were religious works published abroad (a number confiscated from Anne Boleyn), there were numerous classical texts, and many of the non-print items had belonged to the monasteries.

Henry's greatest artistic interest was in music. At death he possessed over three hundred instruments of his own. No mean performer himself on the lute and the virginals, the king studied the organ, then a notoriously difficult instrument. Henry was also a keen singer and a more than competent sight-reader. Unusually for a time when ensemble work was generally left to professionals, Henry played the recorder and he and his courtiers sang together. He also composed. Neither of the masses he wrote has survived but thirty-three of his other pieces are known, all but one secular. He was much applauded, but modern research has established that many of his compositions are, effectively, arrangements of continental originals. Henry also employed about sixty professional musicians, a minority of whom worked in the privy chamber while the rest provided music outdoors or in large gatherings. As the reign progressed the king began to employ instrumental groups to perform in the latest style. Most players came from abroad where the skills needed to make and play consorts (sets) of instruments were more advanced. One family, the Bassanos, served the court until the civil war. Henry also cherished the choir of the chapels royal and sought talent for it everywhere, even poaching from Wolsey. Not that the duties of the five men and ten boys were exclusively liturgical, since they acted as extras in royal pageants and disguisings.

Henry VIII: an assessment

That the reign of Henry VIII was enormously significant is beyond question. His rejection of western Christendom in favour of a national church, the mortal wound he gave to traditional Christian life in England, his effective toleration and even promotion of moderate religious reform, his plundering and subsequent liquidation of the accumulated wealth of the church, the innovative use of statute and the resulting change in the qualitative role and importance of parliament, all these left a deeper mark on English history than any monarch since the Norman conquest and any who have followed him. Even more profound has been the consequence of Henry's decision to require, for the first time ever, that subjects should accept belief as defined by the state. From that point on it ceased to be sufficient any longer to offer the crown loyalty and ability; the monarch needed to search hearts. Ideological conformity and non-conformity became substantial and permanent features of English life.

Many historians from the Victorian period and later have wanted to go beyond this factual record. J. A. Froude's monumental *History of England from the Fall of Wolsey to the Defeat of the Spanish Armada* (1858–70) cast Henry as a hero, a statesman of destiny, the father of his people who led them out of medieval darkness towards their worldwide (and Victorian) destiny as 'top nation'. S. R. Gardiner was less effusive but just as convinced of Henry's distinctiveness. He claimed that with no army to back him, Henry's power necessarily 'rested entirely upon public opinion'; 'his strength was in the main the result of his representative character' (Gardiner, 1.6, 11). A. F. Pollard's monumental biography took much the same line. Henry was not only a man of courage in the right place at the right time, but someone who had a deep symbiotic relationship with the people of England and an astute, perhaps instinctive, identification with the contemporary *zeitgeist*. He embodied the national will. That in making omelettes Henry smashed a large number of valuable eggs was beside the point; the alternative would have been civil strife and bloodshed on a huge scale. Other writers have gone even further, claiming that Henry changed the mindset of the nation by embodying in his person 'a self-contained, self-sufficing sovereign *imperium*' which produced 'in the minds of his subjects a new conception of the state', and touched 'their imaginations in a way that no English king had done before' (Morris, 102–3).

Over the years, however, the voices in favour of Henry VIII have not been in a majority. Herbert of Cherbury, writing

in the reign of Charles I, emphasized Henry's paranoia—
'impressions privately given him by any court-whisperer were
hardly or never effaced'—and he remarked that respect for
Henry, both on the continent and at home, disappeared so
rapidly 'that it may truly be said, all his pomp died with
him' (Herbert, 747). Seventeenth- and eighteenth-century religious controversy focused particularly on Henry's motives in
breaking with Rome and dissolving the monasteries, a deli-
cate area for defenders of the protestant establishment. Bishop
Gilbert Burnet argued that defective though Henry was, God
used him to achieve his will. This was hardly a good enough
response when, following the Relief Acts, Roman Catholic pub-
licists sought to advance their claim for complete emancipation
by representing the Reformation as a wrong to be righted.
Henry's actions brought no spiritual benefits to the country;
they were driven by lust and greed. Non-Catholics too accepted
the charge. William Cobbett declared 'It was not a reformation but a devastation of England' (Cobbett, 19). The advent
of the Tractarian movement produced writers from within the
Church of England who also wanted to disavow the past. Thus
Canon R. W. Dixon was a competent historian but nevertheless
explained the Reformation as the work of:

> a man of force without grandeur: of great ability, but not of
> lofty intellect: punctilious yet unscrupulous: centred in him-
> self: greedy and profuse: cunning rather than sagacious: of
> fearful passion and intolerable pride, but destitute of ambi-
> tion in the nobler sense of the word: a character of degraded
> magnificence. (Dixon, 1.4)

More recent scholarship has not been flattering either. J. J.
Scarisbrick emphasized the negative: 'rarely, if ever, have
the unawareness and irresponsibility of a king proved more
costly of the material benefit of his people' (Scarisbrick,

Henry VIII, 526). L. B. Smith stressed the king's lack of consistency. A view that sees Henry as undoubtedly in personal charge of his kingdom but heavily dependent on others and frequently influenced by the balance of factions at court has received strong support. G. R. Elton even concluded that the king was far from masterfully competent or invariably in charge. True, a minority including L. B. Smith has tried to argue that Henry genuinely dominated both court and government and that factions, in so far as they existed, followed his lead. However, it is a fallacy to imagine that dominance and malleability cannot co-exist. The object of a faction was to influence the king as he was making his decision. Henry's subjects had no doubt that this was a real possibility and many lived, and some even died, by that belief. Instead of Henry VIII governing according to his autonomous will, government action emerged from the shifting political and personal context around him.

All this is very evident in the central issues of the reign, the divorce, the breach with Rome, and the royal supremacy. Henry certainly worked at his Great Matter, but to get anywhere he had to rely on others. The theory of royal supremacy was developed by a think-tank of scholars; exploiting these ideas through the medium of parliament required the political skills of Thomas Cromwell, and for courage the king relied on Anne Boleyn.

As this example shows, Henry VIII's policies were essentially personal and not, *pace* his admirers, conceived of in the national interest. Pollard's picture of a king galvanizing the national will needs to be upended: the nation was galvanized to express the king's will. In foreign affairs, where Henry was most continuously and most personally active, he again followed the devices and desires of his own heart. Before 1527 the object was to establish his credentials as a monarch of European standing. From 1527 policy became dominated by the king's Great Matter and the need to protect the action he had taken. There was no other reason for a break with Rome. Having no male heir was dangerous, but Henry's myopic efforts to displace Mary and ignore James of Scotland simply made matters worse. Henry's promotion of religious reform may have had the effect of preventing religious war in England, but whatever Froude and Pollard imagined, this was never in the king's mind. As for the 1540s, the revival of Henry's personal obsession with winning territory in France led him to mishandle the opportunity presented by the victory at Solway Moss and the accession of the infant Mary to the Scottish throne, and so throw away a chance to bring about a peaceful union of Great Britain.

Henry VIII's monumental selfishness was disguised by highly effective propaganda. Holbein's great painting in the privy chamber at Whitehall extolled Henry's achievement in driving out the unworthy and restoring true religion. The frontispiece to the Great Bible, set up in each parish church, is dominated by a Henry declaring 'I make decree that in every dominion of my kingdom men tremble and fear before the living God'—a God who is allowed to peep in at the edge to say 'I have found a man after my own heart who will do my will'. The proclamation of May 1544 which set in hand the swindle of debasement was announced as a move to protect the supply of bullion, made by a king 'tendering above all things the wealth and enriching of this his realm and people' (Hughes and Larkin, 1.328). In 1545, the bill to enact what was the heaviest tax demand of the reign was disguised as 'a poor token of our true and faithful hearts' towards a king who 'has preserved us for almost these forty years' (37 Hen. VIII c. 25).

This modern critical assessment would, however, not have been endorsed by Henry VIII's loyal subjects. For them, whatever they might like or loathe in his policies, Henry was everything a king should be; he had all the monarchical virtues in full measure. The first was magnificence, immediately obvious in his personal appearance, whether excelling in the joust before a crowd of courtiers and commoners or grandly robed to dominate a diplomatic set piece. The reputation of the Field of Cloth of Gold spread throughout Europe, not simply as a vastly expensive exercise in image building, but as regal glory in action. Then there were his palaces. The *pièce de résistance* of Henry's Nonsuch challenge to François I was a great statue of Henry himself, with Edward beside him.

A second contemporary royal virtue was military power and success; apostles of peace like Erasmus and Zwingli were very much in the minority. Henry's fascination with military technology, most notably heavy guns on board ship and the consequent need to encourage cannon-founding, was entirely in the kingly tradition. So was war. No one was allowed to forget Henry's triumph at the battle of the Spurs, even though it was a skirmish fought in his absence. His armies not only won massive victories which culled two generations of Scottish nobles; in 1544 they savaged the lives of ordinary Scots and ruined the lowland economy. Supremely, with the capture of Boulogne, Henry became the only king to win territory in France for more than a century. A taste for building and a taste for war came together in his huge programme of coastal fortification after 1539, and the creation of the best navy in Atlantic waters. If Henry was not the first warrior of Europe, it was not for want of trying.

The third thing which impressed Henry's people was his personality. More than fifty years after his death, London's Fortune Theatre could put on a play with the simple title *When you See Me you Know Me* and be sure that the public would know who was meant, and even that an audience would recognize Henry's mannerisms on stage. The performance was such a hit that Shakespeare's company had to reply with *Henry VIII*. Thanks to printing, and particularly the mandatory availability of the Great Bible, Henry was almost certainly the first English monarch whose likeness his subjects could recognize. Popular ballads celebrated Henry's fame, while in political circles he was a byword for how a king should be obeyed. His daughter Mary, faced with the tendency of her masculine courtiers to treat the orders of a queen regnant as an invitation to debate, declared that 'she only wished [her father] might come to life again for a month' (*CSP Spain*, 1554, 167).

Henry's personality has continued to impress to the present day, even inspiring a popular Victorian music-hall song. One reason for this was his continuing relevance to ongoing protestant/Catholic controversy. Another factor was the theatre, in particular Shakespeare's *Henry VIII*. Continuously popular in the seventeenth and eighteenth centuries and also frequently performed in the nineteenth, the play attracted all the great actors, though more for the role of Wolsey than for Henry himself. This, in turn, led to scenes from the play becoming popular subjects for painters, and Victorian book illustrators followed. The illustrations by Joseph Nash to his four-volume *The Mansions of England in the Olden Time* (1839–49) are a notable example; the set was reissued three times, the last as late as 1912. Historical novelists also focused on Henry, such as William Harrison Ainsworth in *Windsor Castle* (1843) and

Ford Madox Ford in *The Fifth Queen* (1906–8) and many more subsequently.

Shakespeare's *Henry VIII* with its emphasis on pageantry went out of fashion in the twentieth century, but pageantry and costume coupled with the drama of Henry's private life made the king an obvious subject for the cinema. Pride of place must go to *The Private Life of Henry VIII* (1933) which won an Oscar for Charles Laughton as the king, though at the cost of implanting in the mind of every viewer a fallacious conception of Tudor table manners. Richard Burton's playing of Henry in *Anne of the Thousand Days* (1969) was colourless and there is little to be said for James Robertson Justice in *The Sword and the Rose* (1953) or for the various versions of the *Prince and the Pauper*. The farcical *Carry on Henry* (1971), with Sidney James, is notable only as the most widely seen treatment of Henry VIII. Probably because a series allows for a longer treatment, Henry has been better served by television, both in presentations (for example, by David Starkey) and dramatizations. The BBC series, *The Six Wives of Henry VIII* (1972), was a brilliant evocation of the claustrophobia of the Tudor court and Keith Michell portrayed a Henry who developed and aged in ways entirely credible. The transfer to the cinema, *Henry VIII and his Six Wives* (1972) was not successful. However, all these pieces concentrate on the domestic Henry. Robert Bolt's play about Sir Thomas More, *A Man for All Seasons* (1960, filmed 1966) is of quite another order, setting out to face the issues of the 1530s head on. The result is a brilliant study of conscience in an amoral world, which succeeds by underplaying not only More's own moral ambivalence, but also the complexity of the character of Henry VIII (played in the film by Robert Shaw), the reality of the royal conscience, and the fact that the divorce was an issue of huge national significance.

Judged for more than his private life and the contemporary values of magnificence, military prowess, and 'force' or personality, Henry VIII's enduring achievement was to uncover the power of the English crown. Thomas More had advised Thomas Cromwell to 'ever tell [the king] what he ought to doe but never what he is able to doe...for if [a] Lion knew his owne strength, harde were it for any man to rule him' (Roper, ed. Hitchcock, 56–7). Under Henry VIII parliament did his will; the great of the land walked wary of him; he laid the ghost of Thomas Becket; local franchises were brought to heel; he had wealth greater than any previous monarch. Most significant of all, Henry annexed to himself a theocratic kingship which was distinctive and personal. What the break with Rome established in England was not 'Catholicism without the pope' but the king as pope. Not that Henry claimed the sacramental powers of the pontiff, but what he did claim was absolute spiritual sovereignty in England, even to the point of defining what the English must believe.

That this exalting of the status of the English monarchy was Henry's own achievement there can be no doubt, even though it should probably be put down to instinct more than thought, and it certainly needed other minds to rationalize and develop it. Nevertheless, the driving force was Henry's personal awareness of his own unique status, of what it meant to be king. Nor is this entirely attributable to his quarrel with Rome, although the opposition he met then did force him to push back the limitations on his identity even further. As early as 1515 he had declared in *Hunne's Case*: 'By the ordinance of God we are King of England, and kings of England in time past have never had any superior but God only' (Ogle, 153). Three years later he dismissed the ancient claim of Westminster Abbey to be a permanent sanctuary for offenders as a travesty of what the Anglo-Saxon kings and 'holy popes' had intended, and announced that he would unilaterally sweep away 'the abuses which have encroached and have the matter reduced to the true intent of the original makers' (72 English Reports 369). In his first attempt to stabilize English rule in Ireland he reminded his lieutenant, the earl of Surrey, that as 'sovereign lord and prince ... of our absolute power we be above the laws' (*State Papers, Henry VIII*, 3.53).

Henry VIII's achievement was, thus, to aggregate to his person—and to exercise directly—more authority than any previous English king. After him—in some ways because of him—government would become steadily bigger, more bureaucratic, and unavoidably less personal. In politics, royal initiative would retreat before the need to sustain consensus among an élite which could exploit parliament to assert an increasing voice. 'The supreme head of the church of England' would shrink to a 'supreme governor of this realm as well in all spiritual or ecclesiastical causes as temporal'. Henry VIII's reign, in other words, saw the apogee of personal monarchy in England.

Sources

W. Harrison Ainsworth, *Windsor Castle* (1843) · M. Bateson, 'Notes and documents: Aske's examination', *English Historical Review*, 5 (1890), 550–73 · C. G. Bayne and W. H. Dunham, eds., *Select cases in the council of Henry VII*, Selden Society, 75 (1958) · R. Bolt, *A man for all seasons* (1960) · G. Burnet, *The history of the Reformation of the Church of England*, ed. N. Pocock, 7 vols. (1865) · *CSP Spain* · *CSP Milan* · *CSP Venice* · G. Cavendish, *The life and death of Cardinal Wolsey*, ed. R. S. Sylvester, Early English Text Society, original ser., 243 (1959) · M. A. S. Hume, ed. and trans., *Chronicle of King Henry VIII of England* (1889) · W. Cobbett, *A history of the protestant Reformation* (1850) · H. M. Colvin, D. R. Ransome, J. Summerson, and others, *The history of the king's works*, 3–4 (1975–82) · *Correspondencia de Gutierre Gómez de Fuensalida*, ed. duque de Berwick y de Alba (Madrid, 1907) · *Writings and disputations of Thomas Cranmer*, ed. J. E. Cox, Parker Society, [17] (1844) · A. G. Dickens, *Reformation studies* (1982) · E. Sturtz and V. Murphy, eds., *Divorce tracts of Henry VIII* (Angers, 1988) · R. W. Dixon, *History of the Church of England* (1878–1902) · G. Bray, ed., *Documents of the English Reformation* (1994) · M. H. Dodds and R. Dodds, *The Pilgrimage of Grace, 1536–1537, and the Exeter conspiracy, 1538*, 2 vols. (1915) · *Literary remains of King Edward the Sixth*, ed. J. G. Nichols, 2 vols., Roxburghe Club, 75 (1857) · G. R. Elton, *The Tudor constitution*, 2nd edn (1982) · *English historical documents*, 5, ed. C. H. Williams (1967) · *The English reports*, 178 vols. (1900–32) · F. Madox Ford, *The fifth queen* (1906–8) · *The acts and monuments of John Foxe*, ed. S. R. Cattley, 8 vols. (1837–41) · J. A. Froude, *History of England*, 12 vols. (1856–70) · S. R. Gardiner, *Students' history of England*, 3 vols. (1895) · Great Bible (1539) · E. Hall, *The union of the two noble and illustre famelies of Lancastre & Yorke*, ed. H. Ellis (1809) · J. Bain, ed., *Hamilton papers*, 2 vols. (1890–92) · E. Herbert, *The history of England under Henry VIII*, ed. White Kennett (1870) · *The manuscripts of his grace the duke of Rutland*, 4 vols., Historical Manuscripts Commission, 24 (1888–1905) · D. Starkey, ed., *The inventory of King Henry VIII: the transcript* (1998) · T. A. Lacey, ed., *The King's Book*, Church Historical Society, new ser. (1932) · The King's Primer (1545) · *LP Henry VIII*, vols. 1–21 · S. E. Lehmberg, *The Reformation Parliament, 1529–1536* (1970) · S. E. Lehmberg, *The later parliaments of Henry VIII* (1977) · H. Savage, ed., *Love letters of Henry VIII* (1949) · D. MacCulloch, *Thomas Cranmer: a life* (1996) · C. Morris, *The Tudors* (1955) · J. G. Nichols, ed., *Narratives of the days of the Reformation*, Camden Society, old ser., 77 (1859) · J. Nash, *The mansions of England in the olden time*, 4 vols. (1839–49) · B. H. St J. O'Neil, *Castles and cannon* (1960) · A. Ogle, *The tragedy of the Lollards' Tower* (1959) · N. Harpsfield, *The life and death of Sr Thomas Moore, knight*, ed. E. V. Hitchcock, Early English Text Society, original ser., 186 (1932) · R. Pole, *De unitate ecclesiasticae defensione* (1555) · A. F. Pollard, *Henry VIII* (1902) · W. Roper, *The life of Sir Thomas More*, ed. E. V. Hitchcock, Early English Text Society, 197 (1935) · W. Roper, 'The life of Sir Thomas More', *Two early Tudor lives*, ed. R. S. Sylvester and D. P. Harding (1962) · Rymer, *Foedera*, 2nd edn · J. J. Scarisbrick, 'The pardon of the clergy', *Cambridge Historical Journal*, 12 (1956), 22–39 · J. J. Scarisbrick, *Henry VIII* (1968) · W. H. Schenk, *Reginald Pole* (1950) · W. Shakespeare, *Henry VIII* · L. B. Smith, *A Tudor tragedy…Catherine Howard* (1961) · L. B. Smith, *Henry VIII* (1971) · *St German's Doctor and student*, ed. T. F. T. Plucknett and J. Barton, Selden Society, 91 (1974) · *State papers published under…Henry VIII*, 11 vols. (1830–52) · A. Luders and others, eds., *Statutes of the realm*, 11 vols. in 12, Record Commissions (1810–28) · T. Stemmler, *Die Liebesbriefe Heinrichs VIII an Anna Boleyn* (Zürich, 1988) · R. Strong, *Holbein and Henry VIII* (1967) · P. L. Hughes and J. F. Larkin, eds., *Tudor royal proclamations*, 1 (1964) · *Tyndale's works*, ed. H. Walter,

3 vols., Parker Society (1848–50) · D. Wilkins, *Concilia Magnae* *III*
Britanniae (1737) · W. L. Williams, 'The union of England and
Wales', *Transactions of the Honourable Society of Cymmrodorion*
(1907–8), 47–117 · T. Wyatt, *Collected poems*, ed. J. Daadler
(1975)

Index